Thomas Cadell, William Strahan, John Moore, Davies Cadell &

A View of Society and Manners in France, Switzerland and Germany

Vol. 1

Thomas Cadell, William Strahan, John Moore, Davies Cadell &

A View of Society and Manners in France, Switzerland and Germany
Vol. 1

ISBN/EAN: 9783337155353

Printed in Europe, USA, Canada, Australia, Japan

Cover: Foto ©ninafisch / pixelio.de

More available books at **www.hansebooks.com**

A VIEW

OF

SOCIETY AND MANNERS

IN

FRANCE, SWITZERLAND, AND GERMANY:

WITH

ANECDOTES relating to some EMINENT CHARACTERS.

BY JOHN MOORE, M.D.

IN TWO VOLUMES.

VOL. I.

Strenua nos exercet inertia: navibus atque
Quadrigis petimus bene vivere. Quod petis, hic est.
Hor.

The SECOND EDITION, Corrected.

LONDON:
Printed for W. STRAHAN; and T. CADELL, in the Strand.
M DCC LXXIX.

ADVERTISEMENT.

FROM a diffidence of his own abilities, and from other motives not so well founded, the Author of the following Letters thought it expedient, in the first edition, to throw a slight veil over the real situation in which they were written: he imagined also, that by this means some reflections, particularly those on gaming, might be introduced more naturally, and with a stronger effect. But having been assured by those of whose friendship and judgment he is equally convinced, that the assumed character and feigned situation in the two first letters gave an air of fiction to the real incidents in the rest of the work, he has now restored those two letters to their original form.

TO HIS GRACE

DOUGLAS,

Duke of HAMILTON and BRANDON, Marquis of DOUGLAS, &c.

MY LORD DUKE,

ALTHOUGH eſtabliſhed practice might, on this occaſion, juſtify my holding a language to your Grace which I never before uſed, yet you have nothing of that kind to fear; it is as inconſiſtent with my diſpoſition to offer adulation, as it is contrary to yours to deſire it.—Nor does this addrefs proceed from a vain belief that the luftre of your Name will difpofe the Public to wink at the blemifhes of my performance. The higheft titles do not fcreen even thofe to whom they belong from contempt, when their perfonal characters are contemptible; far lefs can they fhelter the dulnefs or folly of others.

I am prompted to offer this View of Society and Manners to your Grace, by fentiments of the moft fincere efteem and attachment; and, exclufive of all confiderations of that nature, it is prefented with peculiar propriety to you, as no other perfon has had equal opportunities of knowing how far the objects it comprehends are juft, and faithfully drawn from nature.

Some

DEDICATION.

Some perhaps may imagine, that I should have displayed more prudence in offering this work to a less competent judge; but I am encouraged in my desire of prefixing your Name to these imperfect Sketches, by the fond persuasion that nobody can be more inclined to afford them the indulgence of which I am sensible they stand in so much need.

I have the honour to be, with the most respectful and cordial regard,

Your Grace's

Most obedient, and

obliged Servant,

THE AUTHOR.

CONTENTS

OF THE

FIRST VOLUME.

LETTER I. p. 1.

LETTER II. p. 11.

Plan of conduct while abroad.—Agree to correspond by letter.—Servants.—Masters.

LETTER III. p. 18.

Marquis de F———.—Colisée—Characters.

LETTER IV. p. 26.

French manners.

LETTER V. p. 33.

Paris.—London.—French opinions.—Marquis de F—— and Lord M——.

LETTER VI. p. 38.

Loyalty, English, German, Turkish, French. —Le Roi.—Princes of the blood.—Ideas of government.

LETTER VII. p. 48.

Sentiments of Frenchmen concerning the British constitution.

LETTER VIII. p. 54.

French Kings have peculiar reasons to love their subjects.—The three sons of Catharine of Medicis.—Henry IV.—Natural effects of exertion and of sloth on the body, understanding, heart.

LETTER IX. p. 63.

A French lover.

LETTER X. p. 68.

Groundless accusations.—Friendship.—English travellers.

LETTER XI. p. 76.

English prejudices.—Conversation with Mr. B——. Reflections.

LETTER XII. p. 86.

Tragedy of Siege of Calais.—Bon mot of Duc d'Ayen.—Russia.—Prussia.—France.—Statue of Lewis XV.—Epigrams.

LETTER XIII. p. 95.

Chevalier B—— and his lady.—Madame de M——, her character;—her misfortune.

LETTER XIV. p. 103.

Condition of the common people in France.—Unwillingness to censure the King.—French parliaments. — Lawyers indiscriminately ridiculed on the French stage.—Opposition in England.

LETTER XV. p. 113.

Dubois and Fanchon.

LETTER XVI. p. 126.

Mankind do not always act from motives of self-interest.—A fine gentleman and a pine-apple.—Supper at the Marquis de F——'s. —Generosity of Mr. B——. Men who calculate.—Men who do not.

LETTER XVII. p. 137.

Different taste of French and English with respect to tragedy.—Le Kain.—Garrick.—French comedy.—Comedie Italienne, Carlin.—Repartée of Le Kain.

LETTER XVIII. p. 150.

Pleasure and business.—Lyons.—Geneva.

LETTER XIX. p. 157.

Situation of Geneva.—Manners.—Government.—The clergy.—Peculiar customs.—Circles.—Amusements.

LETTER XX. p. 168.

English families at Cologny.—Le jour de l'Escalade.—Military establishment.—Political squabbles.—Sentiments of an Englishman.—Of a gentleman of Geneva.

LETTER XXI. p. 178.

King of Arquebusiers.—A Procession.—A Battle.

LETTER XXII. p. 187.

A Feast.

LETTER XXIII. p. 193.

The garrison and fortifications of Geneva not useless.—Standing armies in other countries.—The freedom and independence of Geneva of service to the King of Sardinia.

LETTER XXIV. p. 201.

Journey to the Glaciers of Savoy.—Mole.—Cluse.—The Rhone and the Arve.—Sallenche.—Mules.—A church.—Conversation with a young peasant in the valley of Chamouni.

CONTENTS.

LETTER XXV. p. 214.

Mountanvert.—The Chamois.—Mount Breven.—Mont Blanc.—The Needles.—The Valley of Ice.—Avalanches.

LETTER XXVI. p. 228.

Account of Glaciers continued.—Theories.

LETTER XXVII. p. 236.

Idiots.—The sentiments of an old soldier.—Guatres.—Journey from Chamouni to the Pays de Vallais.—Martigny.—Sion.

LETTER XXVIII. p. 247.

Road to St. Maurice.—Reflections on the situation of the Pays de Vallais.—Bex.—Aigle.—St. Gingo.—Meillerie.—Evian.—Repaille.

CONTENTS.

LETTER XXIX. p. 261.
Voltaire.

LETTER XXX. p. 273.
Voltaire.

LETTER XXXI. p. 286.
The education proper for an English gentleman.

LETTER XXXII. p. 301.
Suicide frequent at Geneva.—Two remarkable instances.

LETTER XXXIII. p. 309.
The Pays de Vaud.—Lausanne.—Vevay.—Ludlow.

LETTER XXXIV. p. 318.
Murat.—Swiss peasants.

LETTER XXXV. p. 325.

Bern.

LETTER XXXVI. p. 335.

Religion.—Government.—Troops.

LETTER XXXVII. p. 345.

Soleurre.—Basil.—Judicious remark on the use of language, by a Dutchman.

LETTER XXXVIII. p. 351.

Manners.—Reflections on formality.—The library.—Holbens.—Arsenal.—Council-hall.—The clock in the Tower.—A head.

LETTER XXXIX. p. 361.

Marechal Contades.——Theatre.——French troops.

LETTER XL. p. 368.

Gothic architecture.—Cathedral of Strasburg.—A sermon.—A Jewish plot.

LETTER XLI. p. 377.

Karlsrutch.—The Margrave of Baden Durlach.

LETTER XLII. p. 387.

Manheim.—The Elector.—The court.—A buffoon.

LETTER XLIII. p. 394.

Heidelberg.—The same church for the Protestant and Roman Catholic worship.—Parade devotion.

LETTER XLIV. p. 399.

Reflections on the liberty of the press.—Comparisons of inconveniencies arising from that

that cauſe with thoſe felt under deſpotic reſtraint.

LETTER XLV. p. 406.

Mentz.

LETTER XLVI. p. 411.

Frankfort.—Lutherans unkind to Calviniſts.—Pſalmody.—Burials.—Jews.

LETTER XLVII. p. 422.

Manners.—Diſtinction of ranks.—Theatrical entertainments.—The German language.—Traineaus.

LETTER XLVIII. p. 433.

Nobility and citizens.—The revenge of a Tobacconiſt.—The field of Bergen.

LETTER XLIX. p. 443.

The Prince of Hesse Darmstadt.—Discipline.—The family of Prince George.

A VIEW

OF

SOCIETY AND MANNERS

IN

France, Switzerland, and Germany.

LETTER I.

Paris.

I Was greatly difappointed by your not coming to town, as you intended, having been for fome time impatient to inform you of what paffed between your young friend —— and me; I relied till the moment of our departure on having an opportunity of doing this perfonally, and I feize the firft occafion of communicating the whole to you, in the only manner now in my power.

You will remember the uneasiness you once expressed to me on account of that gentleman's propensity to gaming, and of the inconveniences to which he had been put by some recent losses; you will also remember the resolutions which, in consequence of your request, he formed against play; but you have yet to learn, that he resumed the dice before the month was ended in which he had determined never to touch them more, and concluded one unfortunate night, by throwing away a sum far exceeding any of his former losses.

Ashamed of his weakness, he carefully concealed his misfortune from you, and thereby has been subjected to some distresses of a more mortifying nature than any he had formerly felt.

What

What shocked him most was a circumstance which will not greatly astonish you—the indifference which many who call themselves his friends showed at his situation, and the coldness with which they excused themselves from making any attempts to relieve him from his difficulties. Several to whom he had advanced considerable sums in the days of his good fortune, declared a perfect inability of repaying any part of their debt; they told some sad tale of an unforeseen accident, which had put that entirely out of their power for the present; yet one of those unfortunate gentlemen, the same evening that he refused to repay our friend, lost double the sum, every farthing of which he actually paid in ready money.

Mr. ——'s expectations from those resources having in a great measure failed, he applied to Mr. P—— in the City, who supplied him with money, at legal interest,

sufficient to clear all his debts, for which he has granted him a mortgage on his estate.—While our young friend informed me of all this, he declared, that the remorse he felt on the recollection of his folly was infinitely greater than any pleasure he had ever experienced from winning, or could enjoy from the utmost success. He expressed, at the same time, a strong sense of obligation to you and to me, for our endeavours to wean him from the habit of gaming, regretted that they had not been sooner successful, but was happy to find, that he still had enough left to enable him to live in a decent manner, agreeable to a plan of œconomy which he has laid down, and to which he is resolved to adhere till the mortgage is relieved. " I have now (added
" he in a solemn manner) formed an ulti-
" mate resolution against gaming for the rest
" of my life; if I ever deviate from this,
" you have a right to consider me as devoid
" of manly firmness and truth, unworthy
" of

" of your friendship, and the weakest of
" mortals."

Notwithstanding the young gentleman's failure on a former occasion, yet the just reflexions he made on his past conduct, and the determined manner in which he spoke, give me great hopes that he will keep his present resolution.—To him I seemed fully persuaded of this, and ventured to say, that I could scarcely regret his last run of bad luck, which had operated so blessed an effect; for he who has the vigour to disentangle himself from the snares of deep play, at the expence of half his fortune, and with his character entire, may on the whole be esteemed a fortunate man. I therefore insisted strongly on the wisdom of his plan, which I contrasted with the usual determination of those who have been unlucky at play. Without fortitude to retrench their expences, or bear their first misfortunes, they can only bring themselves the length of resolving to renounce gaming *as soon as they*

they shall regain what they have lost; and imagining they have still a claim to the money which is now in the pockets of others, becauſe it was once in their own, they throw away their whole fortune in ſearch of an inconſiderable part, and finiſh by being completely ruined, becauſe they could not ſupport a ſmall inconvenience. I pointed out, how infinitely more honourable it was to depend for repairing his fortune on his own good ſenſe and perſeverance, than on the revolutions of chance; which, even if they ſhould be favourable, could only re-eſtabliſh him at the expence of others, moſt probably of thoſe who had no hand in occaſioning his loſſes. His inſeparable companion —— —— entered while I was in the middle of my harangue. Our friend, who had previouſly acquainted him with his determination of renouncing gaming, endeavoured to prevail on that gentleman to adopt the ſame meaſure, but in vain. —— —— laughed at his propoſal, ſaid, " he was too eaſily terrified; that

" one

" one tolerable run of good fortune would
" retrieve his affairs; that my fears about
" ruin were mere bugbears; that the word
" *ruin*, like cannon charged with powder,
" had an alarming found, but was attended
" with no danger; that if the worft fhould
" happen, I could be but ruined; which was
" only being in the fame fituation with
" fome of the moft fafhionable people in
" the nation."

He then enumerated many inftances of thofe who lived as well as the wealthieft men in England, and yet every body pronounced them ruined. " There is Ch——
" F——, added he, a man completely
" ruined; yet beloved by his friends, and
" admired by his country as much as
" ever."

To this fine reafoning I replied, " That
" if nobody had been influenced by that
" gentle-

"gentleman's example, except those who
"possessed his genius, his turn for play,
"would never have hurt one man in the
"kingdom; but that those who owed their
"importance solely to their fortune, ought
"not to risk it so wantonly as he might
"do, whose fortune had always been of
"little importance, when compared with
"his abilities; and since they could not
"imitate Mr. F—— in the things for
"which he was so justly applauded, they
"ought not to follow his example in those
"for which he was as justly condemned;
"for the same fire which burns a piece of
"wood to ashes, can only melt a guinea,
"which still retains its intrinsic value,
"*though his Majesty's countenance no longer
"shines upon it.*"

———— did not seem to relish my argument, and soon after left us; but our young friend seemed confirmed in his resolutions, folutions, and gave me freſh aſſurances, the day on which I left London, that he never would vary.

Knowing the intereſt you take in his welfare, and the high eſteem he has for you, I have thought it right to give you this piece of information which I know will afford you pleaſure. His greateſt difficulty in adhering to the new adopted plan will be at firſt; in his preſent ſtate of mind, the ſoothings and ſupport of friendſhip may be of the greateſt ſervice.

When your affairs permit you to go to London, I dare ſay you will take the earlieſt opportunity of throwing yourſelf in his way: You will find no difficulty in perſuading him to accompany you to the country. Removed for ſome months from his preſent companions and uſual lounging-places, the influence of his old habits will gradually diminiſh; and, confirmed by your converſation,

converſation, ſmall chance will remain of his being ſucked into the old ſyſtem, and again whirled round in the vortex of diſſipation and gaming.

LETTER II.

Paris.

YOUR setting out for London immediately on the receipt of my letter, is what might have been expected.—Nothing renders a man so active as an eager desire of doing good; and I might have foreseen, that you would catch at the opportunity with which I furnished you to indulge a ruling passion.

It gives me great satisfaction to know, that our young friend and you are upon such a confidential footing; and I heartily hope that nothing will interrupt a connection which must be a source of pleasing reflection to you, and in every way advantageous to him.—I had no doubt that he
would

would readily agree to accompany you to the country; but I was not so certain that he might not have found it necessary to accept of your other very friendly proposal.—His refusal is a proof, that he has reconciled his mind to his circumstances; and, with those sentiments, I am convinced that he will be able to live within his remaining yearly income with more satisfaction than he enjoyed when he spent five times that sum.

You insist so much on my writing to you regularly, from the different places where I may reside during my absence from England, that I begin to believe you are in earnest, and shall certainly obey your commands.

I know you do not expect from me a minute account of churches and palaces; However agreeable these may be to the spectator,

spectator, they generally afford but a slender entertainment when served up in description.

There are countries, some of which I may again visit before my return to England, whose appearance always strikes the eye with delight; but it is difficult to convey a precise idea of their beauties in words. The pencil is a more powerful vehicle than the pen for that purpose; for the landscape is apt to vanish from the mind before the description can be read.

The manners, customs, and characters of the people may probably furnish the chief materials, in the correspondence you exact, with such reflections as may arise from the subject. In these, I apprise you before-hand, I shall take what latitude I please: And though the com-

plexion

plexion of my letters may moſt probably receive ſome tint or ſhade of colouring from the country where they may be wrote; yet if I take it into my head to inſiſt on the little tricks of an attorney, when you expect to hear of the politics of a prime miniſter; or, if I tell you a tale about an old woman, when you are impatient for anecdotes of a great general, you muſt not fret or fall into a paſſion; for if you do not permit me to write on what ſubjects I pleaſe, and treat them in my own way, the correſpondence you require would become a ſad ſlavery to me, and of conſequence no amuſement to you. Whereas, if you leave me free and unreſtrained, it will at leaſt form ſome occupation to myſelf, may wean me from the habit of lounging, and will afford an excuſe, in my own mind, for my leaving thoſe parties of pleaſure where people are apt to continue, forcing smiles, and yawning spontaneously, for two or three hours after all relish is fled.

Yet in this dismal condition many remain night after night, because the hour of sleep is not yet arrived;—and what else can they do?

Have you never found yourself in this listless situation? Without any pleasure where you are, without any motive to be gone, you remain in a kind of passive, gaping oyster-state, till the tide of the company moves you to your carriage. And when you recover your reflection in your bed-chamber, you find you have passed the two last hours in a kind of humming buzzing stupor, without satisfaction, or ideas of any kind.

I thank you for your offer of Dupont. Knowing your regard for him, and his dexterity and intelligence in the science

of

of valet-de-chambrefhip, I fee the full force of the facrifice you are willing to make. If I could be fo felfifh on another occafion as to accept your offer, the good-will I bear to your old friend John would prevent me at prefent. Dupont, to be fure, is worth twenty of John for that employment; but I can never forget his long attachment, and I am now fo habituated to him, that one generally efteemed a more perfect fervant would not fuit me fo well. I think myfelf benefited even by his deficiencies, which have obliged me to do many things for myfelf that other people perform by the hands of their fervants. Many of our acquaintances feem abfolutely incapable of motion, till they have been wound up by their valets. They have no more ufe of their hands for any office about their own perfons, than if they were paralytic. At night they muft wait for their fervants, before they can undrefs themfelves, and go to bed: In the morning, if the valet happen to be out of the way, the mafter muft remain helplefs and fprawling in bed, like a turtle on its back upon the kitchen-table of an alderman.

I remain, &c.

LETTER III.

Paris.

I Went a few nights since to the Italian Comedy; while I enjoyed the exquisite *naiveté* of my old friend Carlin, the Marquis de F——, whom you have seen at London, entered the box:—He flew to me with all the vivacity of a Frenchman, and with every mark of pleasure and regard. He had ten thousand questions to ask about his friends in England all in one breath, and without waiting for an answer. Mon cher ami this, ma chere amie t'other; la belle such a one, la charmante such another.

Perceiving we disturbed the company, and having no hopes that the Marquis would be more quiet for some time, I proposed

poſed leaving the Comedy. He aſſented immediately :—Vous avez raiſon : il n'y a perſonne ici ; c'eſt un deſert—(by the way, the houſe was very much crowded)— Je ſuis venu comme vous voyez en po- liſſon;—tout le monde eſt au Coliſſée— Allons.—We ſtepped into his vis-à-vis: He ordered the coachman to drive vite comme tous les diables. The horſes went as faſt as they could, and the Marquis's tongue ſtill faſter than they.

When we arrived, I propoſed going up to the gallery, where we might ſee the company below, and converſe without in- terruption. Bon, ſays he, nous nous nicherons dans un coin pour critiquer tout le monde, comme deux diables boi- teux.

A lady of a fine ſhape and majeſtic air drew my attention : I aſked the Marquis if he did not think her remarkably handſome?

fome?—Là, là, faid he, coldly.—Nous fommes heureufement placés pour elle. C'eft un tableau fait pour être vu de loin. —I then took notice of the exceffive whitenefs of her fkin.——C'eft apparement le gout de fon amant d'aujourd'hui, faid he; et quand un autre fe prefenteroit qui prefere la couleur de puce, à l'aide d'un peu de l'eau chaude, elle feroit auffi fon affaire.

I next remarked two ladies dreffed a little beyond the extravagance of the mode. Their features betrayed the approach of fifty, in fpite of all the art which had evidently been ufed to conceal that hated age.

At fight of them the Marquis ftarted up. Ah! parblieu, faid he, ces deux morceaux d'antiquité font de mes parentes.— Excufez moi pour deux minutes: il faut que je m'approche d'elles, dans le deffein de les féliciter de leurs appas. Old ladies, continued

continued he, who have the rage to be thought young, are of all animals the moſt vindictive when neglected, and I have particular reaſons for wiſhing to remain in their good graces. He then left me, and having walked round the circle with the ladies, returned and took his ſeat. I have got myſelf well out of the ſcrape, ſaid he; I told them I was engaged with a Milord, whom I ſhould have the honour of preſenting at their houſe; and I fixed a young officer with them, whoſe beſt hopes of promotion depend upon their influence at court, and who dares as ſoon quit his colours in battle, as forſake theſe two pieces of old tapeſtry till they chuſe to retire.

A young man very magnificently dreſſed entered the room: He announced his importance by his airs, his buſtle, the loud and deciſive tone of his voice. The Marquis told me, it was Monſ. le Duc de ———; that it was indiſpenſably neceſſary that I ſhould

should be presented to him; there was no living at Paris without that advantage; adding,—Il est un peu fat, infiniment bête; d'ailleurs le meilleur enfant du monde.

A fine lady next appeared, who seemed to command the admiration of the whole assembly. She floated round the circle of the Colissée, surrounded by a cluster of Petits Maitres, whose eyes were fixed on her, and who seemed moved by her motion, like satellites under the influence of their planet. She, on her part, was perfectly serene, and unembarrassed by the attention and the eyes of the spectators. She smiled to one, nodded to another, shrugged to a third, struck a fourth with her fan, burst into a fit of laughter to a fifth, and whispered in the ear of a sixth. All these, and a thousand tricks more, she ran through with the ease of an actress and the rapidity of a juggler. She seemed fully persuaded that she was the only person present worthy of attention; that it belonged to her to develope her charms, display her graces and airs; and that it was the part of the rest of the company to remain attentive and admiring spectators.

Cette drolesse là, said the Marquis, est jolie, et pour cette raison on croit qu'elle a de l'esprit: On a même tâché de repeter ses bons mots; mais ils ne sont faits que pour sa bouche. Elle est beaucoup plus vaine que sensible, grand soutien pour sa vertu! au reste, elle est dame de qualité, en faveur de laquelle elle possede un gout de hardiesse si heureux, qu'elle jouit du benefice de l'effronterie sans être effrontée.

I was surprised to find all this satire directed against so beautiful a woman, and suspected that the edge of F——'s remarks was sharpened by some recent pique. I was going to rally him on that supposition, when he fuddenly ſtarted up, ſaying, Voilà Monſ. de ——, le meilleur de mes amis.—Il eſt aimable; on ne peut pas plus,—Il a de l'eſprit comme un démon.—Il faut que vous le connoiſſiez. Allons:—Deſçendons. So ſaying, he hurried me down ſtairs, preſented me to Monſ. de —— as un philoſophe Anglois, who underſtood race-horſes better than the great Newton himſelf, and who had no averſion to the game of Whiſt. Monſ. de —— received me with open arms, and we were intimate friends in ten minutes. He carried the Marquis and me to ſup at his houſe, where we found a numerous company.

The converſation was cheerful and animated. There were ſome very ingenious men preſent, with an admirable mixture of agreeable women, who remained to the laſt, and joined in the converſation even when it turned on ſubjects of literature; upon which occaſions Engliſh ladies generally

rally imagine it becomes them to remain filent. But here they took their fhare without fcruple or hefitation. Thofe who underftood any thing of the fubject delivered their fentiments with great precifion, and more grace than the men; thofe who knew nothing of the matter rallied their own ignorance in fuch a fprightly manner, as convinced every body, that knowledge is not neceffary to render a woman exceedingly agreeable in fociety.

After paffing a moft delightful evening, I returned to my lodgings, my head undifturbed with wine, and my fpirits unjaded by play.

LETTER IV.

Paris.

WE have been a month at Paris; a longer time than was intended at our arrival: yet our departure appears to me at a greater distance now than it did then.

F―― has been my most constant companion; he is universally liked, lives in the very best company, and whoever is introduced by him is sure of a favourable reception. I found little or no difficulty in excusing myself from play. The Marquis undertook to make this matter easy; and nothing can be a greater proof of his influence in some of the most fashionable circles, than his being able to introduce a man without a title, and who never games.

He is alſo intimately acquainted with ſome of the moſt eminent men of letters, to whom he has made me known. Many of thoſe, whoſe works you admire, are received at the houſes of the firſt nobility on the moſt liberal footing.

You can ſcarcely believe the influence which this body of men have in the gay and diſſipated city of Paris. Their opinions not only determine the merit of works of taſte and ſcience, but they have conſiderable weight on the manners and ſentiments of people of rank, of the public in general, and conſequently are not without effect on the meaſures of government.

The ſame thing takes place in ſome degree in moſt countries of Europe; but, if I am not miſtaken, more at Paris than any where elſe; becauſe men of letters are here at once united to each other by the various academies,

academies, and diffused among private societies, by the manners and general taste of the nation.

As the sentiments and conversation of men of letters influence, to a certain degree, the opinions and the conduct of the fashionable world; the manners of these last have a more obvious effect upon the air, the behaviour, and the conversation of the former, which in general is polite and easy; equally purified from the awkward timidity contracted in retirement, and the disgusting arrogance inspired by university honours, or church dignities. At Paris, the pedants of Moliere are to be seen on the stage only.

In this country, at present, there are many men distinguished by their learning, who at the same time are cheerful and easy in mixed company, unpresuming in argument, and in every respect as well bred

bred as those who have no other pretenfion.

Politeness and good manners, indeed, may be traced, though in different proportions, through every rank, from the greateſt of the nobility to the loweſt mechanic. This forms a more remarkable and diſtinguiſhing feature in the French national character, than the vivacity, impetuoſity, and fickleneſs, for which the ancient as well as the modern inhabitants of this country have been noted.—It certainly is a very ſingular phænomenon, that politeneſs, which in every other country is confined to people of a certain rank in life, ſhould here pervade every ſituation and profeſſion. The man in power is courteous to his dependant, the proſperous to the unfortunate, the very beggar who ſolicits charity, does it ' en homme comme il faut;' and if his requeſt be not granted, he is ſure, at leaſt, that it will be refuſed with an appearance of humanity, and not with harshness or insult.

A stranger, quite new and unversed in their language, whose accent is uncouth and ridiculous in the ears of the French, and who can scarcely open his mouth without making a blunder in grammar or idiom, is heard with the most serious attention, and never laughed at, even when he utters the oddest solecism or equivocal expression.

I am afraid, said I, yesterday, to a French gentleman, the phrase which I used just now is not French. Monsieur, replied he, cette expression effectivement n'est pas Françoise, mais elle mérite bien de l'être.

The most daring deviation from fashion, in the important article of dress, cannot make them forget the laws of good-breeding. When a person appears at the public walks,

walks, in clothes made againſt every law of the mode, upon which the French are ſuppoſed to lay ſuch ſtreſs, they do not gaze or ſneer at him; they allow him firſt to paſs, as it were, unobſerved, and do not till then turn round to indulge the curioſity which his uncommon figure may have excited. I have remarked this inſtance of delicacy often in the ſtreets in the loweſt of the vulgar, or rather of the common people; for there are really very few of the natives of Paris, who can be called vulgar.

There are exceptions to theſe, as to all general remarks on the manners and character of any nation.

I have heard inſtances of the military treating poſtillions and inn-keepers with injuſtice; and the ſeigneur or intendant oppreſſing the peaſant. Examples of the abuſe of power, and inſolence of office, are

are to be met with every where. If they are tolerated, the fault lies in the government.

I have not been fpeaking of the French government. Their national character is one thing; the nature of their government is a very different matter. But I am convinced there is no country in Europe where royal favour, high birth, and the military profeffion, could be allowed fuch privileges as they have in France, and where there would be fo few inftances of their producing rough and brutal behaviour to inferiors.

LETTER V.

Paris.

A Candid Englishman, of whatever rank in life he may be, must see with indignation, that every thing in this kingdom is arranged for the accommodation of the rich and the powerful; and that little or no regard is paid to the comfort of citizens of an inferior station. This appears in a thousand instances, and strikes the eye immediately on entering Paris.

I think I have seen it somewhere remarked, that the regular and effectual manner in which the city of London is lighted at night, and the raised pavements on the sides of every street, for the security and conveniency of foot-passengers, seem to indicate,

that the body of the people, as well as
the rich and great, are counted of some
importance in the eye of government.
Whereas Paris is poorly and partially lighted; and except on the Pont Neuf and Pont
Royal, and the keys between them, is not
provided with little walks on the sides of
the streets, for the accommodation and
safety of foot-passengers. They must therefore grope their way as they best can,
and skulk behind pillars, or run into shops,
to avoid being crushed by the coaches,
which are driven as near the wall as the
coachman pleases; dispersing the people
on foot at their approach, like chaff before
the wind.

It must be acknowledged, that monarchy
(for the French do not love to hear it called
despotism, and it is needless to quarrel with
them about a word) is raised in this country so very high, that it quite loses sight of
the bulk of the nation, and pays attention
only

only to a few; who being in exalted stations, come within the Court's sphere of vision.

Le peuple, in France, is a term of reproach.—Un homme du peuple, implies a want of both education and manners. Un homme comme il faut, on the other hand, does not imply a man of sense or principle, but simply a man of birth or fashion; for a man may be homme comme il faut, and yet be devoid of every quality which adorns human nature. There is no question that government leaves the middle and inferior ranks of life in some degree unprotected, and exposed to the injustice and insolence of the great; who are considered in this country, as somewhat above the Law, though greatly below the Monarch.

But the polished mildness of French manners, the gay and sociable turn of the nation, the affable and easy conduct of
masters

masters to their servants, supply the deficiencies, and correct the errors, of the government, and render the condition of the common people in France, but particularly at Paris, better than in several other countries of Europe; and much more tolerable than it would be, if the national character resembled that of those countries.

* * * * * * *

I was interrupted by Lord M. who arrived last night. He agreed to dine with us. F——— called soon after: he was disengaged also, and promised to be of the party.

You know how laborious a thing it is to keep alive a dialogue with my Lord M. The conversation either degenerates into a soliloquy on your part, or expires altogether. I was therefore exceedingly happy with the thoughts of the Marquis's company.

pany. He was uncommonly lively; addreſſed much of his converſation to his Lordſhip; tried him upon every ſubject, wine, women, horſes, politics, and religion. He then ſung Chanſons à boire, and endeavoured in vain to get my Lord to join in the chorus. Nothing would do.— He admired his clothes, praiſed his dog, and ſaid a thouſand obliging things of the Engliſh nation. To no purpoſe; his Lordſhip kept up his ſilence and reſerve to the laſt, and then drove away to the opera.

Ma foi, ſaid the Marquis, as ſoon as he went out of the room, il a de grands talens pour le ſilence, ce Milord là.

LETTER VI.

Paris.

IN a former letter, I mentioned good breeding as a ſtriking part of the French national character. Loyalty, or an uncommon fondneſs for, and attachment to, the perſons of their princes is another.

An Engliſhman, though he views the virtues of his king with a jealous eye during his reign, yet he will do them all juſtice in the reign of his ſucceſſor.

A German, while he is ſilent with reſpect to the foibles of his prince, admires all his talents much more than he would the ſame qualities in any other perſon.

A Turk,

A Turk, or Perſian, contemplates his Emperor with fear and reverence, as a ſuperior being, to whoſe pleaſure it is his duty to ſubmit, as to the laws of Nature, and the will of Providence.

But a Frenchman, while he knows that his king is of the ſame nature, and liable to all the weakneſſes of other men; while he enumerates his follies, and laughs as he laments them, is nevertheleſs attached to him by a ſentiment of equal reſpect and tenderneſs; a kind of affectionate prejudice, independent of his real character.

Roi * is a word which conveys to the minds of Frenchmen the ideas of benevolence, gratitude, and love; as well as thoſe of power, grandeur, and happineſs.

---

* We tranſlate le Roi, by ' the King,' which is by no means equivalent. Le Roi does himſelf, and makes others do, what he pleaſes. The King cannot do what he pleaſes, but does what others pleaſe.

They flock to Versailles every Sunday, behold him with unsated curiosity, and gaze on him with as much satisfaction the twentieth time as the first.

They consider him as their friend, though he does not know their persons; as their protector, though their greatest danger is from an Exempt or Lettre de Cachet; and as their benefactor, while they are oppressed with taxes.

They magnify into importance his most indifferent actions; they palliate and excuse all his weaknesses; and they impute his errors or crimes, to his ministers or other evil counsellors; who (as they fondly assert) have, for some base purpose, imposed upon his judgment, and perverted the undeviating rectitude of his intentions.

They repeat, with fond applause, every saying of his which seems to indicate the
smallest

smallest approach to wit, or even bears the mark of ordinary sagacity.

The most inconsiderable circumstance which relates to the Monarch is of importance: whether he eat much or little at dinner; the coat he wears, the horse on which he rides, all afford matter of conversation in the various societies at Paris, and are the most agreeable subjects of epistolary correspondence with their friends in the provinces.

If he happens to be a little indisposed, all Paris, all France, is alarmed, as if a real calamity was threatened: and to seem interested, or to converse upon any other subject till this has been discussed, would be considered as a proof of unpardonable indifference.

At a review, the troops perform their manœuvres unheeded by such of the spectators as are within sight of the King. They

They are all engroffed in contemplation of their Prince.—Avez vous vu le roi?—— Tenez—ah!—voilà le roi.—Le roi rit.— Apparement il eft content.—Je fuis charmé, —ah, il touffe!—A-t-il touffé?——Oui, parbleu! et bien fort.—Je fuis au défefpoir.

At mafs, it is the King, not the Prieft, who is the object of attention. The Hoft is elevated; but the people's eyes remain fixed upon the face of their beloved Monarch.

Even the moft applauded pieces of the theatre, which in Paris create more emotion than the ceremonies of religion, can with difficulty divide their attention. A fmile from the King makes them forget the forrow of Andromaché, and the wrongs of the Cid.

This exceffive attachment is not confined to the perfon of the Monarch, but extends

to

to every branch of the royal family; all of whom, it is imagined in this country, have an hereditary right to every gratification and enjoyment that human nature is capable of receiving. And if any caufe, moral or phyfical, impede or obftruct this, they meet with univerfal fympathy. The moft trivial difappointment or chagrin which befalls them, is confidered as more ferious and affecting, than the moft dreadful calamity which can happen to a private family. It is lamented as if the natural order of things were counteracted, and the amiable Prince, or Princefs, deprived, by a cruel phæ-nomenon, of that fupreme degree of happinefs, to which their rank in life gives them an undeniable title.

All this regard feems real, and not affected from any motive of intereft; at leaft it muft be fo with refpect to the bulk of the people, who can have no hopes of ever being known to their princes, far lefs

of

of ever receiving any perfonal favour from them.

The philofophical idea, that Kings have been appointed for public conveniency; that they are accountable to their fubjects for mal-adminiftration, or for continued acts of injuftice and oppreffion; is a doctrine very oppofite to the general prejudices of this nation. If any of their kings were to behave in fuch an imprudent and outrageous manner as to occafion a revolt, and if the infurgents actually got the better, I queftion if they would think of new-modelling the government, and limiting the power of the crown, as was done in Britain at the revolution, fo as to prevent the like abufes for the future. They never would think of going further, I imagine, than placing another prince of the Bourbon family on the throne, with the fame power that his predeceffor had, and then quietly lay down their arms, fatisfied with his royal word or declaration to govern with more equity.

The French seem so delighted and dazzled with the luſtre of Monarchy, that they cannot bear the thoughts of any qualifying mixture, which might abate its violence, and render its ardour more benign. They chuſe to give the ſplendid machine full play, though it often ſcorches and threatens to conſume themſelves and their effects.

They conſider the power of the king, from which their ſervitude proceeds, as if it were their own power. You will hardly believe it; but I am ſure of the fact: They are proud of it; they are proud that there is no check or limitation to his authority.

They tell you with exultation, that the king has an army of near two hundred thouſand men in the time of peace. A
French-

Frenchman is as vain of the palaces, fine gardens, number of horſes, and all the parapharnalia belonging to the court of the Monarch, as an Engliſhman can be of his own houſe, gardens, and equipage.

When they are told of the diffuſion of wealth in England, the immenſe fortunes made by many individuals, the affluence of thoſe of middle rank, the ſecurity and eaſy comfortable ſituation of the common people, inſtead of being mortified by the compariſon which might naturally occur to their imaginations, they comfort themſelves with the reflection, that the court of France is more brilliant than that of Great Britain, and that the duke of Orleans and the Prince of Condé have greater revenues than any of the Engliſh nobility.

When they hear of the freedom of debate in parliament, of the liberties taken in writing or ſpeaking of the conduct of

the

the king, or meafures of government, and the forms to be obferved, before thofe who venture on the moſt daring abufe of either can be brought to punifhment, they feem filled with indignation, and fay with an air of triumph, C'eſt bien autrement chez nous : Si le Roi de France avoit affaire à ces Meſſieurs là, il leur enfeigneroit à vivre. And then they would proceed to inform you, that, parbleu! their miniſter would give himfelf no trouble about forms or proofs; that fufpicion was fufficient for him, and without more ado he would fhut up fuch impertinent people in the Baſtile for many years. And then raifing their voices, as if what they faid were a proof of the courage or magnanimity of the miniſter— Ou peut-être il feroit condamner ces droles là aux galères pour la vie.

LETTER VII.

Paris.

IT would be almoſt ſuperfluous to obſerve, that there are a great many people in France, who think in a very different manner from that which I have mentioned in my laſt, and who have juſt and liberal ideas of the deſign and nature of government, and proper and manly ſentiments of the natural rights of mankind. The writings of Monteſquieu are greatly admired: This alone is ſufficient to prove it. Many later authors, and the converſation of the philoſophical and reaſoning people diſplay the ſame ſpirit.

What is mentioned in my laſt letter, however, comprehends the general turn or manner of thinking of the French nation,

tion, and evinces how very oppofite their fentiments upon the fubject of civil government are, to thofe of our countrymen.

I have heard an Englifhman enumerate the advantages of the Britifh conftitution to a circle of French Bourgeois, and explain to them in what manner the people of their rank of life were protected from the infolence of the courtiers and nobility; that the pooreft fhop-keeper, and loweft tradefman in England, could have immediate redrefs for any injury done him by the greateft nobleman in the kingdom.

Well, what impreffion do you think this declamation had upon the French auditory? You will naturally imagine they would admire fuch a conftitution, and wifh for the fame in France:—Not at all. They fympathized with the great: They feemed to feel for their want of importance. One obferved, C'eft peu de chofe d'être noble chez vous; and another, fhaking his head, added, Ce n'eſt pas naturel tout cela.

When mention was made that the king of Great Britain could not impoſe a tax by his own authority; that the conſent of parliament, particularly of the houſe of commons, was neceſſary, to which aſſembly people of their rank of life were admitted; they ſaid with ſome degree of ſatisfaction, Cependant, c'eſt aſſez beau cela. But when the Engliſh patriot, expecting their complete approbation, continued informing them, that the king himſelf had not the power to encroach upon the liberty of the meaneſt of his ſubjects; that if he or the miniſter did, damages were recoverable at a court of law, a loud and prolonged DIABLE iſſued from every mouth. They forgot their own ſituation, and the ſecurity of the people, and turned to their natural bias of ſympathy with the King, who they

all

all seemed to think muſt be the moſt opprefſed and injured of mankind.

One of them at laſt, addreſſing himſelf to the Engliſh politician, ſaid, Tout ce que je puis vous dire, Monſieur, c'eſt que votre pauvre Roi eſt bien à plaindre.

This ſolicitude of theirs for the happineſs and glory of royalty extends in ſome degree to all crowned heads whatever: But with regard to their own monarch, it ſeems the reigning and darling paſſion of their ſouls, which they carry with them to the grave.

A French ſoldier, who lay covered with wounds on the field of Dettingen, demanded, a little before he expired, of an Engliſh officer, how the battle was likely to terminate; and being anſwered, that the Britiſh troops had obtained a great victory; Mon pauvre Roi, ſaid the dying man, que fera-t-il?

For my part, my friend, although I heartily wifh his Majefty all public and domeftic happinefs, yet if the fmalleft folicitude about either fhould difturb my dying moments, it will be the ftrongeft proof that my own affairs, fpiritual and temporal, your concerns, as well as thofe of my other private friends, are in a moft comfortable fituation.

.Adieu.

P. S. I have not feen the Marquis for feveral days. He had informed me, at our very firft meeting, that he was paying his court to a young lady of family, at his mother's defire, who was impatient to fee him married. He faid, he could refufe his mother nothing, parcequ'elle étoit le meilleur enfant du monde: Befides, he faid, the young lady was very pretty and agreeable, and he was over head and ears in love with her. He has told me fince, that every thing was arranged, and he
expected

expected to be in a ſhort time the happieſt man in the world, and would have the honour of preſenting me to his bride very ſoon. I ſhall let you know my opinion of the lady when I ſee her—But let her be what ſhe will, I am ſorry that F—— thinks of marrying ſo early in life; for a Frenchman of five and twenty, is not quite ſo ſedate an animal as an Engliſhman of fifteen.

LETTER VIII.

Paris.

THERE is an abſolute penury of public news. I have nothing particular to inform you of concerning myſelf; but you hold me to my engagement: So here I am ſeated to write to you, without having as yet determined upon a ſubject, in hopes, however, that my pen may gather materials as it moves.

In whatever light this prejudice in favour of monarchy may appear to the eye of philoſophy; and though of all paſſions the love of a King, merely becauſe he is a King, is perhaps the ſillieſt; yet it ſurely ought to be conſidered as meritorious by thoſe who are the objects of it.

No

No people exifting, or who did ever exift, have had fo juft a claim to the gratitude and affections of their fovereign, as the French. They rejoice in his joy, are grieved at his grief, proud of his power, vain of his accomplifhments, indulgent to his failings. They cheerfully yield their own conveniences to his fuperfluities, and are at all times willing to facrifice their lives for his glory.

A King, one would imagine, muft be a perfect monfter of felfifhnefs and infenfibility, who did not love fuch fubjects, and who did not beftow fome time and attention to promote their happinefs: Yet the French nation has not had a Monarch worthy of all this regard fince the days of Henry IV. and of all their kings they ufed him the worft.

Of the three brothers who immediately preceded him, the firft was a fickly creature,

ture, as feeble in mind as in body; the second, a monster of superstition and cruelty; and the third, after a dawn of some brightness, allowed his meridian to be obscured by the grossest clouds of effeminacy and voluptuousness. Their Italian mother, who governed all the three, seems to have been perfectly unrestrained by any feelings of humanity or of conscience, and solely guided by motives of interest, and the most perfidious policy.

The princes who have succeeded, as well as those who reigned before the fourth Henry, serve as foils which display his bright qualities with double lustre.

Notwithstanding all the inducements which the French Kings have to promote the happiness of their subjects, it may be many centuries before they are blessed with one who shall have that passion in such a high degree.

A cha-

A character in which the great and amiable virtues are so finely blended, is very rarely produced in any nation. How small then must be the chance that this prize shall fall to the individual who is destined for the throne? Henry received an education very different from that which is generally bestowed on Kings. His character was formed in the hardy school of adversity: his mind was strengthened by continual exertions of courage and prudence. He was taught humanity by suffering under the rod of tyranny, and experiencing the pangs of the unfortunate. Having frequently stood in need of friends, he knew the value of their attachment, and his heart became capable of friendship.

Difficulties and dangers often strike out particles of genius which otherwise might remain latent and useless, and contribute to the formation of a vigorous character, by animating those sparks of virtue which a
life

life of indolence would have completely extinguished.

Thofe people who, from their earlieſt infancy, have found every thing provided for them, who have not much ambition, and confequently are feldom excited to any great exertion of their faculties, generally feel thefe faculties dwindle and grow weak, for the fame reafon that a man's arms would become gradually feeble, and at length perfectly ufelefs, if he were to wear them in a fcarf for any confiderable time.

That the faculties of the underſtanding, like the finews of the body, are relaxed by floth and ſtrengthened by exercife, nobody will doubt. I imagine the fame analogy holds in fome degree between the body and the qualities of the heart. Benevolence, pity, gratitude, are, I fufpect, exceedingly apt to ſtagnate into a calm, fluggiſh gifh infenfibility in that breaft which has not been agitated by real misfortunes.

People do not fully enter into diftreffes which they never have felt, and which they think they run but a fmall rifk of feeling. Accordingly it has been remarked, that thofe who have been favoured through life with the fmiles of fortune, and whofe time has been fpent in the amufements of courts, and luxurious indulgences, very often acquire an aftonifhing infenfibility to the misfortunes of others. The character the moft perfectly cold of all I ever knew, devoid of friendfhip, gratitude, and even natural affection, belongs to a perfon, whofe life has been a continued feries of fortunate events.

Yet while all their cares are contracted, and all their feelings abforbed, within the compafs of their own fkin, fuch people feem often convinced, that they themfelves

are

are of the most humane dispositions, and the most extensive benevolence, upon no better foundation, than because they have felt themselves affected by the artful distresses of a romance, and because they could shed a few barren tears at a tragedy.

If to these symptoms of sensibility, they can add, that of having occasionally given a guinea when the contribution has been set a going, or have parted with a little superfluous money to free themselves from importunity, they have then carried benevolence to the utmost length of *their* idea of that virtue.

They have no notion of any thing beyond this; nor would they make one active exertion, postpone a single party of pleasure, or in any shape interrupt the tranquillity of their own indolence, to perform the most essential service (I will not
say

say to a friend, such people can have none) to any of the human race.

There are many exceptions, but in general those persons who are exposed to *the slings and arrows of outrageous fortune*, who have experienced the base indifference of mankind, and have in some degree *felt what wretches feel*, are endued with the truest sympathy, and enter, with the most lively sensibility, into the situation of the unfortunate.

Non ignara mali, miseris succurrere disco,

said Dido, who had been obliged to fly from her country, to Æneas, who had been witness to the destruction of his.

Dido and Æneas!—How in the name of wandering have we got into their company? I could no more have guessed at this, than at the subject of one of Montaigne's Essays from the title. We set out,

I believe, with something about France;—but you cannot expect that I should attempt to take up a thread which is left so far behind.

Adieu.

LETTER IX.

Paris.

I Mentioned in a former letter, that my friend F—— was on the point of being married. He called at my lodgings a little while ago. His air was so very gay, that I imagined he had some agreeable news to communicate. Me voilà au défefpoir, mon cher ami, said he, with a loud laugh.—You are the merriest man I ever saw in that situation, said I.—He then informed me, that the old Marquis de P. his mistress's father, had waited on his mother, and, after ten thousand apologies and circumlocutions, had given her to understand, that certain things had intervened, which rendered it impossible that he should ever have the honour of being father-in-law to her son; and requested her to in-

form

form him, how infinitely uneafy he and all his family were, at an incident which deprived them of the pleafure they had propofed to themfelves from that connection. His mother, he faid, had endeavoured to difcover the incident which has produced this fudden alteration;—but to no purpofe.—The old gentleman contented himfelf with affuring her, that the particulars would be equally difagreeable and fuperfluous,—and then took his leave, in the moft polite and affectionate terms that the French language could furnifh him with.

F—— told me all this with an air fo eafy and contented, that I did not well know what to make of it. My dear Marquis, faid I, it is fortunate that I have been miftaken; for you muft know, I had taken it into my head that you were fond of the lady.—You were in the right, my friend, faid he, je l'aimai infiniment.——Comment infiniment; faid I, and yet be fo

merry

merry when you are juſt going to loſe her!——Mais vous autres Anglois, ſaid he, vous avez des idées ſi bizarres :——aimer infiniment, cela veut dire aimer comme on aime,—tout le monde aime ainſi quand ill ne ſe hait pas.——Mais je vous conterai toute l'hiſtoire.

My mother, added he, who is the beſt creature in the world, and whom I love with all my ſoul, told me this marriage would make her quite happy.——All my uncles and aunts, and couſins, for ten generations, told me the ſame. I was informed, over and above, that the lady, her father, and all their relations, wiſhed this alliance, with the moſt obliging earneſtneſs. The girl, herſelf, is tolerably pretty. They will perſuade me to marry ſome time or other, thought I; why not now, as well as at another time? Why ſhould I refuſe to do a thing which will pleaſe ſo many people, without being in

VOL. I. F the

the fmalleft degree difpleafing to myfelf?— To be fure, faid I, that would have been ill-natured. It was lucky, however, that you happened to be perfectly difengaged, and did not prefer any other woman.

You are miftaken, my friend, faid he; I preferred many to the lady in queftion, and one in particular, whofe name I will not mention, but whom I love—whom I do love.——Comme on aime, faid I, interrupting him.——Non, parbleu! added he, with warmth, comme on n'aime pas.——Good Heaven! then, cried I, how could you think of marrying another?— Cela n'empêche rien, faid the Marquis, coolly;——for I could not marry the other. She had the ftart of me, and had undergone the ceremony already; and therefore fhe had no objection to my obliging my mother and relations in this particular, for fhe is the beft-natured woman in the world.

So

So she appears to be, said I.——O, pour cela oui, mon cher, added he, elle est la bonté même. However, I am very well pleased, upon the whole, that the affair has gone off without any fault of mine; and though it is possible that it may be brought on at some future period, I shall still be a gainer, parceque un mariage reculé est toujours autant de gagné sur le repentir. So saying, he wheeled on his heel, humming,

Non, tu ne le mettra pas, Colin, &c.

There's the picture of a French lover for you.——I set down the whole scene, as soon as F—— left me, and so I leave you to make your own reflections.

Adieu.

LETTER X.

Paris.

YOU have often heard the French accused of infincerity, and of being warm in profeffions, but devoid of real friendfhip.

Our countrymen, in particular, are led into this opinion, from the manners in general being more obfequious here, than in England. What Frenchmen confider as common good manners, many Englifhmen would call flattery, perhaps fawning.

Their language abounds in complimental phrafes, which they diftribute with wonderful profufion and volubility; but they intend no more by them, than an Englifhman means when he fubfcribes himfelf

your

your moſt obedient humble ſervant, at the concluſion of a letter.

A Frenchman not only means nothing beyond common civility, by the plentiful ſhower of compliments which he pours on every ſtranger; but alſo, he takes it for granted, that the ſtranger knows that nothing more is meant. Theſe expreſſions are fully underſtood by his own countrymen: he imagines all the world are as well informed; and he has not the ſmalleſt intention to deceive. But if any man take theſe expreſſions in a literal ſenſe, and believes that people are in reality inſpired with friendſhip, or have fallen in love with him at firſt ſight, he will be very much diſappointed; eſpecially if he expects ſtrong proofs of either.

Yet he has no right to accuſe the French of inſincerity, or breach of friendſhip.—— Friendſhip is intirely out of the queſtion.

They never intended to convey any other idea, than that they were willing to receive him on the footing of an acquaintance;——and it was the bufinefs of his language-mafter to have informed him of the real import of their expreffions.

If the fame words indeed were literally tranflated into Englifh, and ufed by one Englifhman to another, the perfon to whom they were addreffed, would have good reafon to imagine that the other had a particular regard for him, or meant to deceive him; becaufe the eftablifhed modes of civility and politenefs in England do not require fuch language.

The not making a proper allowance for different modes and ufages which accident has eftablifhed, is one great caufe of the unfavourable and harfh fentiments, which the people of the different countries of the

the world too often harbour againſt each other.

You may ſay, perhaps, that this ſuperfluity of compliments which the French make uſe of, is a proof of the matter in queſtion; that the French have leſs ſincerity than their neighbours. By the ſame rule we muſt conclude, that the common people of every nation, who uſe few complimental phraſes in their diſcourſe, have a greater regard to truth, and ſtronger ſentiments of friendſhip, than thoſe in the middle and higher ranks. But this is what I imagine it would be difficult to prove.

Theſe complimental phraſes, which have crept into all modern languages, may, perhaps, be ſuperfluous; or, if you pleaſe, abſurd: but they are ſo fully eſtabliſhed, that people of the greateſt integrity muſt uſe them, both in England and in France;

with

with this difference, that a fmaller proportion will do in the language of the one
country, than in that of the other; but they
are indications of friendfhip in.neither.

Friendfhip is a plant of flow growth, in
every climate. Happy the man who can
rear a few, even where he has the moft
fettled refidence. Travellers, paffing through
foreign countries, feldom take time to cultivate them; if they be prefented with
fome flowers, although of a flimfy texture
and quicker growth, they ought to accept
of them with thankfulnefs, and not quarrel with the natives, for choofing to retain the other more valuable plant for their
own ufe.

Of all travellers, the young Englifh nobility and gentry have the leaft right to
find fault with their entertainment while
on their tours abroad; for fuch of them as
fhow a defire of forming a connection with
the

the inhabitants, by even a moderate degree of attention, are received upon eafier terms than the travellers from any other country. But a very confiderable number of our countrymen have not the fmalleft defire of that nature: they feem rather to avoid their fociety, and accept with reluctance every offer of hofpitality. This happens partly from a prejudice againft foreigners of every kind; partly from timidity or natural referve; and in a great meafure from indolence, and an abfolute deteftation of ceremony and reftraint. Befides, they hate to be obliged to fpeak a language of which they feldom acquire a perfect command.

They frequently, therefore, form focieties or clubs of their own, where all ceremony is difmified, and the greateft eafe and latitude allowed in behaviour, drefs, and converfation. There they confirm each other in all their prejudices, and with united

united voice condemn and ridicule the cuſ-
toms and manners of every country but
their own.

By this conduct the true purpoſe of travelling is loſt or perverted; and many Engliſh travellers remain four or five years
abroad, and have ſeldom, during all this
ſpace, been in any company, but that of
their own countrymen.

To go to France and Italy, and there
converſe with none but Engliſh people, and
merely that you may have it to ſay that
you have been in thoſe countries, is certainly abſurd: Nothing can be more ſo, except to adopt with enthuſiaſm the faſhions,
fopperies, taſte, and manners of thoſe
countries, and tranſplant them to England,
where they never will thrive, and where
they always appear aukward and unnatural.
For after all his efforts of imitation, a travelled Engliſhman is as different from a
French-

Frenchman or an Italian, as an Englifh maftiff is from a monkey or a fox: And if ever that fedate and plain meaning dog fhould pretend to the gay frifkinefs of the one, or to the fubtilty of the other, we fhould certainly value him much lefs than we do.

But I do not imagine that this extreme is by any means fo common as the former. It is much more natural to the Englifh character to defpife foreigners than to imitate them. A few tawdry examples to the contrary, who return every winter from the continent, are hardly worth mentioning as exceptions.

LETTER XI.

Paris.

YOUR acquaintance B—— has been in Paris for these three weeks paſt. I cannot conceive how he has remained ſo long; for he has a very bad opinion of this nation, and is fraught with the ſtrongeſt prejudice againſt French manners in general: He conſiders all their politeſſe as impertinence, and receives their civilities as a prelude to the picking of his pocket.

He and I went this forenoon to a review of the foot-guards, by Marſhal Biron. There was a crowd; and we could with difficulty get within the circle ſo as to ſee conve-

conveniently. An old officer of high rank touched fome people who ftood before us, faying,—Ces deux Meſſieurs font des étrangers ; upon which they immediately made way, and allowed us to pafs.—Don't you think that was very obliging? faid I.—Yes, anfwered he ; but, by heavens, it was very unjuſt.

We returned by the Boulevards, where crowds of citizens, in their holiday dreſſes, were making merry; the young dancing cotillons, the old beating time to the muſic, and applauding the dancers, all in a carelefs oblivion of the paſt, thoughtlefs of the future, and totally occupied with the prefent.—Thefe people feem very happy, faid I.—Happy! exclaimed B——; if they had common fenfe or reflection, they would be miferable. Why fo?—Could not the miniſter, anfwered he, pick out half a dozen of them, if he pleafed, and clap them into

the

the Bicetre?—That is true indeed, said I; that is a cataftrophe which, to be fure, may very probably happen, and yet I thought no more of it than they.

We met, a few days after he arrived, at a French houfe where we had both been invited to dinner. There was an old lady of quality prefent, next to whom a young officer was feated, who paid her the utmoft attention.——He helped her to the difhes fhe liked, filled her glafs with wine or water, and addreffed his difcourfe particularly to her.—What a fool, fays B——, does that young fellow make of the poor old woman! If fhe were my mother, d—n me, if I would not call him to an account for it.——

Though B—— underftands French, and fpeaks it better than moft Englifhmen, he had no relifh for the converfation, foon left the company, and has refufed all invitations

tions to dinner ever fince. He generally finds fome of our countrymen who dine and pafs the evening with him at the Parc Royal.

After the review this day, we continued together, and being both difengaged, I propofed, by way of variety, to dine at the public ordinary of the Hôtel de Bourbon. He did not like this much at firft.—I fhall be teafed, fays he, with their confounded ceremony:—But on my obferving, that we could not expect much ceremony or politenefs at a public ordinary, he agreed to go.

Our entertainment turned out different, however, from my expectations and his wifhes: A marked attention was paid us the moment we entered; every body feemed inclined to accommodate us with the beft places. They helped us firft, and all the company feemed ready to facrifice every
little

little conveniency and diftinction to the ftrangers: For, next to that of a lady, the moft refpected character at Paris is that of a ftranger.

After dinner, B—— and I walked into the gardens of the Palais Royal.

There was nothing real in all the fufs thofe people made about us, fays he.

I can't help thinking it fomething, faid I, to be treated with civility and apparent kindnefs in a foreign country—by ftrangers who know nothing about us, but that we are Englifhmen, and often their enemies.

But their politenefs confifts in trifles, faid he.—In what confifts any body's politenefs? rejoined I.—— The utmoft a Frenchman will do for you, added he, is to endeavour to amufe you, and make your time pafs agreeably while you remain in his country. And I think that no trifle,

anfwered

anſwered I.—There are ſo many ſources of uneaſineſs and vexation in this life, that I cannot help having a good will, and even gratitude, to all thoſe who enable me to forget them:—For ſuch people alleviate my pain, and contribute to my happineſs.

But theſe Frenchmen, rejoined he, do not care a farthing for you in their hearts. —And why ſhould I care a farthing for that? ſaid I.—We have nothing to do with their hearts—You do not expect a friend in every agreeable acquaintance.

But they are an intereſted ſet of people; and even thoſe among them who pretend to be your friends,—do it only for ſome ſelfiſh end.

That is only an aſſertion, ſaid I, but no proof.—If you ſtood in need of pecuniary aſſiſtance, they would not advance you a louis to ſave you from a jail, continued he.

I hope

I hope never to be perfectly afcertained of that, faid I;—but if we were to cultivate friendſhip from the idea of affiſtance of that nature, it would be doing exactly what you accufe them of: Befides, continued I, the power and opportunity of obliging our acquaintances and friends with great, and, what are called, effential fervices, feldom occur; but thofe attentions and courtefies, which fmooth the commerce between man and man, and fweeten focial life, are in every body's power, and there are daily and hourly occafions of difplaying them,—particularly to ſtrangers.———Curfe their courtefies, faid he, they are the greateſt *Bore* in nature.—I hate the French.— They are the enemies of England, and a falfe, deceitful, prefidious— But as we did not come over, interrupted I, to fight them at prefent, we fhall fufpend hoſtilities till a more convenient feafon; and in the mean time, if you have no objection, let us go to the play.

He

He agreed to this propofal, and here our converfation ended.

You know B—— is as worthy a fellow as lives; and, under a rough addrefs, conceals the beft difpofition in the world. His manner, I imagine, was originally affumed from a notion, which he has in common with many people, that great politenefs, and apparent gentlenefs of behaviour, are generally accompanied with falfehood and real coldnefs;—even inhumanity of character,—as if human nature, like marble, took a polifh proportionable to its hardnefs.

This idea is certainly formed without an accurate examination, and from a fuperficial view of mankind. As a boorifh addrefs is no proof of honefty, fo is politenefs no indication of the reverfe;—and if they are once reduced to an equality in thefe particulars, it is evident that the latter is preferable in every other refpect.

But to return to the French, I am clearly of opinion, that a stranger may fairly avail himself of every conveniency arising from their obliging manners, although he should be convinced that all their assiduity and attention are unconnected with any regard to him, and flow entirely from vanity and self-love. He may perceive that his Parisian friend, while he loads him with civilities, is making a display of his own proficiency in the science of politeness, and endeavouring to thrust himself forward in the good opinion of the company, by yielding the preference on a thousand trifling occasions:—Though he plainly sees, that all this stooping is with a view to conquer, why should he repine at a victory which is accompanied with so many conveniencies to himself? why quarrel with the motive while he feels the benefit of the effect?

If writers or preachers of morality could, by the force of eloquence, eradicate selfish-
nefs

nefs from the hearts of men, and make them in reality love their neighbours as themfelves, it would be a change devoutly to be wifhed. But until that bleffed event, let us not find fault with thofe forms and attentions which create a kind of artificial friendfhip and benevolence, which for many of the purpofes of fociety produce the fame effects as the true.

People who love to amufe themfelves with play, and have not ready money, are obliged to ufe counters. You and I, my friend, as long as we cut and fhuffle together, fhall never have occafion for fuch a fuccedaneum;—I am fully perfuaded we are provided, on both fides, with a fufficient quantity of pure gold.

LETTER XII.

Paris.

WHEN B—— and I went to the play-house, as was mentioned in my laſt, we found a prodigious crowd of people before the door: We could not get a place till after a conſiderable ſtruggle. The play was The Siege of Calais, founded on a popular ſtory, which muſt needs be intereſting and flattering to the French nation.

You cannot conceive what preſſing and crowding there is every night to ſee this favourite piece, which has had the ſame ſucceſs at Verſailles as at Paris.

There are ſome few critics, however, who aſſert that it is entirely devoid of merit, and owes its run to the popular nature

of

of the fubject, more than to any intrinfic beauty in the verfes, which fome declare are not even good French.

When it was laft acted before the King, it is faid, his Majefty, obferving that the Duc d'Ayen did not join in applauding, but that he rather fhewed fome marks of difguft, turned to the Duke and faid, Vous n'applaudiffez pas? Vous n'étes pas bon François, Monfieur le Duc:—To this the Duke replied,—à Dieu ne plaife que je ne fuffe pas meilleur que les vers de la piéce.

Obedient to the court in every other particular, the French difregard the decifions pronounced at Verfailles in matters of tafte. It very often happens that a dramatic piece, which has been acted before the royal family and the court, with the higheft applaufe, is afterwards damned with every circumftance of ignominy at Paris. In all works of genius the Parifians lead the judgment of the courtiers, and dictate to their monarch.

In other countries of Europe, it has happened, that some Prince of superior talents has, by the brightness of his own genius, enlightened the minds of his subjects, and dispelled the clouds of barbarism from his dominions.

Since the commencement of this century, a great empire has been improved from a state of gross ignorance, refined by the arts of peace, and instructed in the arts of war, by the vast genius and industry of one of its Princes, who laid the foundation of its present power and grandeur.

Another inconsiderable state, with fewer resources, has, at a later period, been created a powerful monarchy, by the astonishing efforts, perseverance, and magnanimity of its present king; whose love of
know-

knowledge and the arts has drawn some of the greatest geniuses in Europe to his capital; whence science and taste must gradually flow through his whole dominions, where they were formerly but little cherished.

In these instances, and others which might be enumerated, the princes have been superior in genius to any of their subjects. The throne has been the source whence knowledge and refinement have flowed to the extremities of the nation.

But this has never been the case in France, where it is not the king who polishes the people;—but the people who refine the manners, humanize the heart, and, if it be not perfectly opaque, enlighten the understanding of the king.

Telemaque, and many other works, have been composed with this intention. In
many

many addreſſes and remonſtrances to the throne, excellent precepts and hints are inſinuated in an indirect and delicate manner.

By the emphatic applauſe they beſtow on particular paſſages of the pieces repreſented at the theatre, they convey to the monarch the ſentiments of the nation reſpecting the meaſures of his government.

By aſcribing qualities to him which he does not poſſeſs, they endeavour to excite within his breaſt a deſire to attain them: they try to cajole him into virtue. Conſidered in this point of view, the deſign of the equeſtrian ſtatue which the city of Paris has erected in honour of Lewis XV. may have been ſuggeſted from a more generous motive than flattery, to which it is generally imputed. This was begun by Bouchardon; who died when the work

was

was well advanced, and has since been committed to Pigal to be finished.

The horse is placed on a very high pedestal. At the angles, are four figures, standing in the manner of Caryatides, who represent the four virtues, Fortitude, Justice, Prudence, and the love of Peace. All the ornaments are of Bronze.

The two small sides of the pedestal are ornamented with gilded laurels and inscriptions. On the front, towards the Thuilleries, is the following:

LUDOVICO XV.
OPTIMO PRINCIPI
QUOD
AD SCALDUM, MOSAM, RHENUM,
VICTOR
PACEM ARMIS
PACE
SUQRUM ET EUROPÆ
FELICITATEM
QUÆSIVIT.

The

The large fides of the pedeftal are adorned with trophies and bas reliefs. One reprefents Lewis giving peace to Europe;
the other reprefents him in a triumphal
chariot, crowned by Victory, and conducted
by Renown to a people who fubmit.

When we recollect that the infcription
and emblems allude to the conclufion of
the war before the laft, and what kind of
infcriptions are ufually put under the ftatues
of kings, we fhall not find any thing out-
rageoufly flattering in the above; the moral of which is, that the love of peace is
one of the greateft virtues a king can poffefs——The beft moral that can be in-
finuated into the breaft of a monarch.

In this work the horfe is infinitely more
admired, by fculptors and fatirifts, than
the king. But the greateft overfight is,
that the whole group, though all the figures
are larger than life, have a diminutive

appear-

appearance in the centre of the vast area in which they are placed.

The wits of Paris could not allow such an opportunity of indulging their vein to escape unimproved. Many epigrams are handed about.—Here are two:

> Bouchardon est un animal,
> Et son ouvrage fait pitié;
> Il place les vices à cheval,
> Et met les vertus à pied.

> Voilà notre Roi comme il est à Versailles,
> Sans foi, sans loi, et sans entrailles.

Both are too severe; giving the idea of wicked dispositions, and cruelty of temper, which do not belong to Lewis the Fifteenth; whose real character, in three words, is, that of a good-natured, easy-tempered man, sunk in sloth and sensuality.

I have feen another infcription for the ftatue handed about; it is in Latin, and very fhort.

STATUA STATUÆ.

You may imagine that the authors of thefe would meet with a dreadful punifhment, if they were difcovered. No danger of that kind is fufficient to reftrain the inhabitants of this city, from writing and fpreading fuch pafquinades, which are greatly relifhed by the whole nation.

Indeed, I imagine there is more of the fpirit of revenge, than of good policy, in attempting to repel fuch humours; which, if they did not get vent in this manner, might break out in a more dangerous fhape.

Adieu.

LETTER XIII.

Paris.

I Dined yesterday with an equal number of both sexes, at the Chevalier B—'s. He is F———'s very intimate friend, and has a charming house within a few leagues of Paris, which the Marquis makes full as much use of as the owner.

The Chevalier has a considerable revenue, which he spends with equal magnificence and œconomy. He has been married many years to his present lady, a most agreeable woman, with whom he possesses every thing which can make their union happy, except children. They endeavour to forget this disagreeable circumstance, by a constant succession of company; and, which is very fingular here, the fociety entertained by the hufband and wife are the fame.

F——, though much younger than either, is a great favourite of both; and they are always pleafed when he invites a fmall company of his friends to dine at their houfe.

The prefent party had been propofed by Madame de M——, a rich young widow, much admired here; of whom I fhall give you a glimpfe, en paffant——for do not imagine I undertake to defcribe the moft undefcribable of all human beings,——a fine French lady.

Madame de M—— has fome wit, more beauty, and a greater fhare of vivacity than of both:—if there were a fourth degree of comparifon, I fhould place her vanity there. She laughs a great deal, and fhe is in the right; for her teeth are remarkably fine.

She talks very much, and in a loud and deci-
five tone of voice.—This is not fo judicious,
becaufe her fentiments are not fo brilliant as
her teeth, and her voice is rather harfh.—
She is received with attention and refpect
every where;—that fhe owes to her rank.—
She is liked and followed by the men; this
fhe owes to her beauty. She is not difliked
by the women, which is probably owing
to her foibles.

This lady is thought to be fond of
F―――: fo, to prevent fcandal, fhe defired me to call at her houfe, and attend
her to the Chevalier's.

I found her at her toilette, in confulta-
tion with a general officer and two abbes,
concerning a new head-drefs which fhe had
juft invented.—It was fmart and fanciful;
and, after a few corrections, received the
fanction of all thofe critics. They declared
it to be a valuable difcovery, and foretold
that

that it would immediately become the general mode of Paris, and do immortal honour to the genius of Madame de M——.

She wheeled from before the mirror, with an air of exultation.—Allons, donc, mes enfans —— à la gloire, — cried she; and was proceeding to give orders for her equipage, when a servant entered, and informed her, that Madame la Comtesse had accepted her invitation, and would certainly do herself the honour of dining with her.

I despair of giving you an idea of the sudden change which this message occasioned in the features of Madame de M—. Had she heard of the death of her father, or her only child, she could not have been more confounded.—Est il possible (said she, with an accent of despair) qu'on puisse être si bête!—The servant was called, and examined regarding the import of the answer

he

he had brought from Madame la Comteſſe.
—It was even ſo——ſhe was aſſuredly to
come.—Freſh exclamations on the part of
Madame de M——. Did you ſend to invite her for this day, ſaid I ?—Undoubtedly
I did, replied Madame de M——. That
could be delayed no longer.—She came to
town laſt Sunday.—I therefore ſent her the
politeſt meſſage in the world, begging to
have the honour of her company for this
day, at dinner; and behold, the horrid
woman (with a rudeneſs, or ignorance of
life without example) ſends me word ſhe
will come.

It is very ſhocking, indeed, ſaid I, that
ſhe ſhould have miſunderſtood your kind-
neſs ſo prodigiouſly.—Is it not, ſaid ſhe?
Could any mortal have expected ſo barba-
rous a return of civility?——She is connected with ſome of my relations in the
country:—when ſhe came to town, I immediately left my name with her porter.—

She called next day on me—I had informed my Swifs, that I was always to be out when she came. I was denied accordingly.—Celà eft tout fimple, et felon les régles. The woman is twenty years older than I, and we muft be infupportable to each other.—She ought to have feen, that my invitation was dictated by politenefs only:—the fame politenefs on her part fhould have prompted her to fend a refufal. In this manner we might have vifited each other, dined and fupped together, and remained on the moft agreeable footing imaginable through the whole courfe of our lives:—but this inftance of grofiereté muft put an end to all connection.——Well— there is no remedy:—I muft fuffer purgatory for this one day. Adieu.—Prefent my compliments to Madame B—. Inform her of this horrid accident.

Having condoled with Madame de M— on her unmerited misfortune, I took my leave

leave and joined F——, to whom I recounted the sad chance which had deprived us of that lady's company.

He did not appear quite so unhappy as she had on the occasion; but he swore he was convinced that the Countess had accepted the invitation to dinner par pure malice; for, to his knowledge, she was acquainted with their party to the Chevalier B——'s, and had certainly seized that opportunity of plaguing Madame de M—, whom she hated. Without that douceur, he imagined, the dinner would be as great a purgatory to the Countess, as it could possibly be to Madame de M——. How these affectionate friends contrived to pass their time together I know not, but we had a most agreeable party at the Chevalier's—The Marquis entertaining the company with the history of Madame M—'s misfortune, and the loving tête à tête which it had occasioned.——This he related

lated with such sprightliness, and described his own grief and disappointment with such a flow of good humour, as in some degree indemnified the company for the lady's absence.

LETTER XIV.

Paris.

THOUGH the gentlenefs of French manners qualifies in fome degree the feverity of the government; as I obferved in a former letter, ftill the condition of the common people is by no means comfortable.

When we confider the prodigious refources of this kingdom; the advantages it enjoys above almoft every other country in point of foil, climate, and fituation; the induftry and ingenuity of the inhabitants, attached by affection to their Kings, and fubmiffive to the laws; we naturally expect that the bulk of the nation fhould be at their eafe, and that poverty fhould be as little known here as in any country of Europe.

Europe. I do not speak of that ideal or comparative poverty, the child of envy and covetousness, which may be felt by the richest citizens of London or Amsterdam; or of the poverty produced in capitals by gaming, luxury, and dissipation: But of that actual poverty, which arises when the laborious part of a nation cannot acquire a competent share of the necessaries of life by their industry.

The two first flow from the vices and extravagance of individuals :—The other from a bad government.

Much of the first may be found in London, where more riches circulate than in any city of Europe; of the last there is little to be seen in the country of England.

The reverse of this is the case in France, where the poorest inhabitants of the capital are often in a better situation than the
laborious

laborious peafant. The former by adminiftering to the luxuries, or by taking advantage of the follies of the great and the wealthy, may procure a tolerable livelihood, and fometimes make a fortune; while the peafant cannot, without much difficulty, earn a fcanty and precarious fubfiftence.

To have an adequate idea of the wealth of England, we muft vifit the provinces, and fee how the nobility, the gentry, and efpecially the farmers and country people in general live. The magnificence of the former, and the abundance which prevails among the latter claffes, muft aftonifh the natives of any other country in Europe.

To retain a favourable notion of the wealth of France, we muft remain in the capital, or vifit a few trading or manufacturing towns; but muft feldom enter the chateau of the Seigneur, or the hut of the peafant. In the one, we fhall find nothing but

but tawdry furniture, and from the other we shall be scared by penury.

A failure of crops, or a careless administration, may occasion distress and scarcity of bread among the common people at a particular time: But when there is a permanent poverty through various reigns, and for a long tract of years, among the peasantry of such a country as France; this seems to me the surest proof of a careless, and consequently an oppressive government. Yet the French very seldom complain of their government, though often of their governors; and never of the King, but always of the minister.

Although the enthusiastic affection which the people of this nation once felt for their present monarch be greatly abated, it is not annihilated. Some of the courtiers indeed, who are supposed to administer to the King's pleasures, are detested. The imprudent

dent oftentatious luxury of the miftrefs, is publicly execrated; but their cenfure of the King, even where they think themfelves quite fafe, never burfts out as it would in fome other nations, in violent expreffions, fuch as, Curfe his folly,—his weaknefs, or—his obftinacy. No: Even their cenfure of him is inttermingled with a kind of affectionate regret.—Naturellement il eft bon, they fay.—And when they obferve the deplorable anxiety and difguft in his countenance, wlhich are the concomitants of a conftitution jaded by pleafure, and of a mind incapable of application, they cry, Mon Dieu, qu'il eft trifte!—Il eft malheureux lui-même;——comment peut il penfer à nous autres?

I am perfuaded, that, in fpite of the difcontent which really fubfifts at prefent in France, the King might recover the efteem and affection of his fubjects at once by the fimple manœuvre of difmiffing his minifter, and a few other unpopular characters. A Lettre de cachet, ordering them to banifhment, or fhutting them up in the Baftile, would be confidered as a complete *revolution* of government, and the nation would require no other *Bill of Rights* than what proceeded from this dreadful inftrument of tyranny.

As matters are at prefent, in my opinion, no body of men in France has, properly fpeaking, any rights. The Princes, the nobleffe, and the clergy, have indeed certain privileges which diftinguifh them in different degrees from their fellow-fubjects: but as for rights, they have none; or, which amounts to the fame thing, none which can defend them, or which they can defend againft the Monarch, whenever he in his royal wifdom choofes to invade or annihilate them.

A French-

A Frenchman will tell you, that their parliaments have the right of remonſtrating to the throne upon certain occaſions.—This is a precious privilege indeed! the common-council of London are in poſſeſſion of this glorious right alſo, and we all know what it avails. It is like the power of which Owen Glendower boaſted——" calling ſpirits from the vaſty deep."—But the misfortune was, that none came in conſequence of his call.

The parliaments of Paris can indeed remonſtrate; and have done it with ſuch ſtrength of reaſoning and energy of expreſſion, that if eloquence were able to prevail over unlimited power, every grievance would have been redreſſed.

Some of theſe remonſtrances diſplay not only examples of the moſt ſublime and pathetic eloquence, but alſo breathe a ſpirit of freedom which would do honour to a Britiſh Houſe of Commons.

The

The refiftance which the members of the parliament of Paris made to the will of the King, does them the greateft honour. Indeed the lawyers in France have difplayed more juft and manly fentiments of government, and have made a nobler ftruggle againft defpotic power, than any fet of men in the kingdom. It has therefore often affected me with furprife and indignation, to obferve the attempts that are made here to turn this body of men into ridicule.

One of this profeffion is never introduced on the ftage but in a ridiculous character. This may give fatisfaction to the prince, whofe power they have endeavoured to limit, or to thoughtlefs flavifh courtiers; but ought to be viewed with horror by the nation, for whofe good the gentlemen of the long-robe have hazarded fo much; for in their oppofition to the court, much perfonal danger was to be feared, and no lucrative advantage to be reaped.

Thofe

Those who oppose the court measures in our island incur, I thank Heaven, no personal risk on that account.——A member of the British parliament may launch his patriotic bark in the most perfect security: —He may glide down the current of invective, spread all his canvas, catch every gale, and sail for an hour or two upon the edge of treason, without any risk of being sucked into its whirlpool. But though he has nothing to fear, it is equally evident that he has nothing to hope from such a voyage. Opposition was formerly considered as a means of getting into power: Mais nous avons changé tout cela. Let any one recollect the numbers who, with very moderate abilities, have crawled on their knees into office, and compare them with the numbers and success of those who, armed with genius and the artillery of eloquence, attempt the places by storm; if, after this, he joins the assailants, he must either act from other motives than those of self-interest,

rest, or betray his ignorance in the calculation of chances.

The security, and even the existence, of the parliament of Paris, depending entirely on the pleasure of the King, and having no other weapons, offensive or defensive, but justice, argument, and reason, their fate might have been foreseen—the usual fate of those who have no other artillery to oppose to power:—The members were disgraced, and the parliament abolished. The measure was considered as violent; the exiles were regarded as martyrs; the people were astonished and grieved. At length, recovering from their surprise, they dissipated their sorrow, as they do on all occasions of great calamity,——by some very merry songs.

LETTTER XV.

Páris.

MY friend F—— called on me a few days fince, and as foon as he underftood that I had no particular engagement, he infifted that I fhould drive fomewhere into the country, dine tête-à-tête with him, and return in time for the play.

When we had drove a few miles I perceived a genteel-looking young fellow, dreffed in an old uniform. He fat under a tree, on the grafs, at a little diftance from the road, and amufed himfelf by playing on the violin. As we came nearer we perceived he had a wooden leg, part of which lay in fragments by his fide.

What do you there, foldier? faid the Marquis.—I am on my way home to my own village, mon officier, faid the foldier. —But, my poor friend, refumed the Marquis, you will be a furious long time before you arrive at your journey's end, if you have no other carriage befides thefe, pointing at the fragments of his wooden leg.— I wait for my equipage and all my fuite, faid the foldier; and I am greatly miftaken if I do not fee them this moment coming down the hill.

We faw a kind of cart, drawn by one horfe, in which was a woman, and a peafant who drove the horfe.—While they drew near, the foldier told us he had been wounded in Corfica—that his leg had been cut off—that before fetting out on that expedition, he had been contracted to a young woman in the neighbourhood—that the marriage had been poftponed till his return;——but when he appeared with a
wooden

wooden leg, that all the girl's relations had oppofed the match.—The girl's mother, who was her only furviving parent, when he began his courtfhip, had always been his friend; but fhe had died while he was abroad.—The young woman herfelf, however, remained conftant in her affections, received him with open arms, and had agreed to leave her relations, and accompany him to Paris, from whence they intended to fet out in the diligence to the town where he was born, and where his father ftill lived :——That on the way to Paris his wooden leg had fnapped, which had obliged his miftrefs to leave him, and go to the next village in queft of a cart to carry him thither, where he would remain till fuch time as the carpenter fhould renew his leg.—C'eft un malheur, concluded the foldier, mon officier, bien-tôt reparé — et voici mon amie!———

The girl sprung before the cart, seized the outstretched hand of her lover, and told him with a smile full of affection,—— that she had seen an admirable carpenter, who had promised to make a leg that would not break, that it would be ready by to-morrow, and they might resume their journey as soon after as they pleased.

The soldier received his mistress's compliment as it deserved.

She seemed about twenty years of age, a beautiful, fine shaped girl——a Brunette, whose countenance indicated sentiment and vivacity.

You must be much fatigued, my dear, said the Marquis.——On ne se fatigue pas, Monsieur, quand on travaille pour ce qu'on aime, replied the girl.—The soldier kissed her hand with a gallant and tender air.— When a woman has fixed her heart upon a man,

man, you fee, faid the Marquis, turning to me, it is not a leg more or lefs that will make her change her fentiments.—Nor was it his legs, faid Fanchon, which made any impreffion on my heart. If they had made a little, however, faid the Marquis, you would not have been fingular in your way of thinking; but, allons, continued he, addreffing himfelf to me.——This girl is quite charming—her lover has the appearance of a brave fellow;——they have but three legs betwixt them, and we have four; —if you have no objection, they fhall have the carriage, and we will follow on foot to the next village, and fee what can be done for thefe lovers.—I never agreed to a propofal with more pleafure in my life.

The foldier began to make difficulties about entering into the vis-à-vis.—Come, come, friend, faid the Marquis, I am a Colonel, and it is your duty to obey: Get in without more ado, and your miſtreſs ſhall follow.

Entrons, mon bon ami, ſaid the girl, ſince theſe gentlemen inſiſt upon doing us ſo much honour.

A girl like you would do honour to the fineſt coach in France. Nothing could pleaſe me more than to have it in my power to make you happy, ſaid the Marquis.—Laiſez moi faire, mon Colonel, ſaid the ſoldier. Je ſuis heureuſe comme une reine, ſaid Fanchon.—Away moved the chaiſe, and the Marquis and I followed.

Voyez vous, combien nous ſommes heureux nous autres François à bon marché, ſaid the Marquis to me, adding with a ſmile, le bonheur, à ce qu'on m'a dit, eſt plus cher en Angleterre. But anſwered I; how long will this laſt with theſe poor people?—Ah, pour le coup, ſaid he, voilà
une

une reflexion bien Angloife—that, indeed, is what I cannot tell; neither do I know how long you or I may live; but I fancy it would be great folly to be forrowful through life, becaufe we do not know how foon misfortunes may come, and becaufe we are quite certain that death is to come at laſt.

When we arrived at the inn to which we had ordered the poſtilion to drive, we found the foldier and Fanchon. After having ordered fome victuals and wine—Pray, faid I to the foldier, how do you propofe to maintain your wife and yourfelf?—One who has contrived to live for five years on foldier's pay, replied he, can have little difficulty for the reſt of his life.——I can play tolerably well on the fiddle, added he, and perhaps there is not a village in all France of the fize, where there are fo many marriages as in that in which we are going to fettle——I fhall never want employment.

―――And I, said Fanchon, can weave hair nets and silk purses, and mend stockings. Besides, my uncle has two hundred livres of mine in his hands, and although he is brother-in-law to the Bailiff, and *volontiers brutal*, yet I will make him pay it every sous—And I, said the soldier, have fifteen livres in my pocket; besides two louis that I lent to a poor farmer to enable him to pay the taxes, and which he will repay me when he is able.

You see, Sir, said Fanchon to me, that we are not objects of compassion.――May we not be happy, my good friend (turning to her lover with a look of exquisite tenderness), if it be not our own fault?――If you are not, ma douce amie! said the soldier with great warmth, je ferai bien à plaindre――I never felt a more charming sensation.—The tear trembled in the Marquis's eye.――Ma foi, said he to me, c'est une comédie larmoyante――Then, turning

to

to Fanchon, Come hither, my dear, faid he, till fuch time as you can get payment of the two hundred livres, and my friend, here recovers his two louis, accept of this from me, putting a purfe of louis into her hand—I hope you will continue to love your hufband, and to be loved by him.— Let me know from time to time how your affairs go on, and how I can ferve you. This will inform you of my name, and where I live. But if ever you do me the pleafure of calling at my houfe at Paris,— be fure to bring your hufband with you; for I would not wifh to efteem you lefs or love you more than I do this moment. Let me fee you fometimes; but always bring your hufband along with you.——I fhall never be afraid to truft her with you, faid the foldier:—She fhall fee you as often as fhe pleafes, without my going with her.

It was by too much venturing (as your ferjeant told me) that you loft your leg,
my

my best friend, said Fanchon, with a smile to her lover. Monsieur le Colonel n'est que trop aimable. I shall follow his advice literally, and when I have the honour of waiting on him, you shall always attend me.

Heaven bless you both, my good friends, said the Marquis; may he never know what happiness is who attempts to interrupt your felicity.——It shall be my business to find out some employment for you, my fellow-soldier, more profitable than playing on the fiddle. In the mean time, stay here till a coach comes, which shall bring you both this night to Paris; my servant shall provide lodgings for you, and the best surgeon for wooden legs that can be found. When you are properly equipped, let me see you before you go home. Adieu, my honest fellow; be kind to Fanchon: She seems to deserve your love. Adieu, Fanchon; I shall be happy to hear that

you

you are as fond of Dubois two years hence as you are at prefent. So faying, he fhook Dubois by the hand, faluted Fanchon, pufhed me into the carriage before him, and away we drove.

As we returned to town, he broke out feveral times into warm praifes of Fanchon's beauty, which infpired me with fome fufpicion that he might have further views upon her.

I was fufficiently acquainted with his free manner of life, and I had a little, before feen him on the point of being married to one woman, after he had arranged every thing, as he called it, with another.

To fatisfy myfelf in this particular, I queftioned him in a jocular ftyle on this fubject.

No,

No, my friend, faid he, Fanchon fhall never be attempted by me.——Though I think her exceedingly pretty, and of that kind of beauty too that is moſt to my taſte; yet I am more charmed with her conſtancy to honeſt Dubois, than with any other thing about her:—If fhe loſes that, fhe will loſe her greateſt beauty in my eyes. Had fhe been fhackled to a moroſe, exhauſted, jealous fellow, and defired a redreſs of grievances, the caſe would have been different; but her heart is fixed upon her old lover Dubois, who feems to be a worthy man, and I dare fay will make her happy. If I were inclined to try her, very probably it would be in vain:—The conſtancy which has ſtood firm againſt abſence, and a cannon-ball, would not be overturned by the airs, the tinſel, and the jargon of a petit maitre.——It gives me pleaſure to believe it would not, and I am determined never to make the trial.

F———

F—— never appeared so perfectly amiable.

B—— called and supped with me the same evening. I was too full of the adventure of Fanchon and Dubois not to mention it to him, with all the particulars of the Marquis's behaviour.———This F—— of yours, said he, is an honest fellow. Do—contrive to let us dine with him to-morrow.———By the bye, continued he after a little pause, are not those F——'s originally from England?—I think I have heard of such a name in Yorkshire.

Adieu.

LETTER XVI.

Paris.

I Am uneasy when I hear people assert, that mankind always act from motives of self-interest. It creates a suspicion that those who maintain this system, judge of others by their own feelings. This conclusion, however, may be as erroneous as the general assertion; for I have heard it maintained (perhaps from affectation) by very disinterested people, who, when pushed, could not support their argument without perverting the received meaning of language.—Those who perform generous or apparently disinterested actions, say they, are prompted by selfish motives——by the pleasure which they themselves feel.—— There are people who have this feeling so strong, that they cannot pass a miserable object

object without endeavouring to assist him.—Such people really relieve themselves when they relieve the wretched.

All this is very true: but is it not a strange assertion, that people are not benevolent, because they cannot be otherwise?

Two men are standing near a fruit-shop in St. James's street. There are some pine-apples within the window, and a poor woman, with an infant crying at her empty breast, without. One of the gentlemen walks in, pays a guinea for a pine-apple, which he calmly devours; while the woman implores him for a penny, to buy her a morsel of bread—and implores in vain: not that this fine gentleman values a penny; but to put his hand in his pocket would give him some trouble;——the distress of the woman gives him none. The other man happens to have a guinea in his pocket also;

alſo; he gives it to the woman, walks home, and dines on beef-ſteaks, with his wife and children.

Without doing injuſtice to the taſte of the former, we may believe, that the latter received the higher gratification for his guinea.——You will never convince me, however, that his motive in beſtowing it was as ſelfiſh as the other's.

Some few days after the adventure I mentioned in my laſt letter, I met F——— and B—— at the opera. They had become acquainted with each other at my lodgings two days before, according to B——'s deſire.—It gave me pleaſure to ſee them on ſo good a footing.

F——— invited us to go home and ſit an hour with him before we went to bed; —to which we aſſented.

The

The Marquis then told us, we should have the pleasure of seeing Fanchon, in her best gown, and Dubois, with his new leg— for he had ordered his valet to invite them, with two or three of his companions, to a little supper.

While the Marquis was speaking, his coach drove up to the door of the opera— where a well-known lady was at that moment waiting for her carriage.

B—— seemed to recollect himself of a sudden, saying, he must be excused from going with us, having an affair of some importance to transact at home.

The Marquis smiled——shook B—— by the hand—saying, c'est apparemment quelque affaire qui regarde la constitution, vivent les Anglois pour l' amour patriotique.

When we arrived at the Marquis's, the ſervants and their gueſts were aſſembled in the little garden behind the hotel, and dancing, by moon-light, to Dubois's muſic.

He and Fanchon were invited to a glaſs of wine in the Marquis's parlour.—The poor fellow's heart ſwelled at the ſight of his benefactor.——He attempted to expreſs his gratitude; but his voice failed, and he could not articulate a word.

Vous n'avez pas à faire a des ingrats, Monſieur le Colonel, ſaid Fanchon. My huſband, continued ſhe, is more affected with your goodneſs, than he was by the loſs of his leg, or the cruelty of my relations.——She then, in a ſerious manner, with the voice of gratitude, and in the language of Nature, expreſſed her own and her huſband's obligations to the Marquis; and, amongſt others, ſhe alluded to twenty louis
which

which her hufband had received *de fa part* that very afternoon.——You intend to make a faint of a finner, my dear, faid the Marquis, and to fucceed the better, you invent falfe miracles. I know nothing of the twenty louis you mention.——But I know a great deal; for here they are in my pocket, fays Dubois.—The Marquis ftill infifted they had not come from him.—— The foldier then declared, that he had called about one o'clock, to pay his duty to Monfieur de F——; but not finding him at home, he was returning to his lodgings, when, in the ftreet, he obferved a gentleman looking at him with attention, who foon accofted him, demanding if his name was not Dubois? If he had not loft his leg at Corfica? and feveral other queftions, which being anfwered in the affirmative, he flipped twenty louis into his hand, telling him that it would help to furnifh his houfe.——Dubois in aftonifhment had exclaimed—Mon Dieu! voilà encore Monfieur de F———. Upon which the ftranger had replied:—Yes, he fends you that, by me: and immediately he turned into another ftreet, and Dubois faw no more of him.

We were all equally furprifed at the fingularity of this little adventure. On enquiring more particularly about the appearance of the ftranger, I was convinced he could be no other than B———.

I remembered he had been affected with the ftory of Dubois when I told it him. You know B— is not one of thofe, who allow any emotions of that nature to pafs unimproved, or to evaporate in fentiment. He generally puts them to fome practical ufe.—So having met Dubois accidentally in the ftreet, he had made him this fmall prefent, in the manner, above related; and on his underftanding that Dubois and Fanchon were at F———'s, he he had declined going, to avoid any explanation on the fubject.

Had our friend B—— been a man of fyftem, or much reflection, in his charity, he would have confidered, that as the foldier had already been taken good care of, and was under the protection of a generous man, there was no call for his interfering in the bufinefs; and he would probably have kept his twenty guineas for fome more preffing occafion.

There are men in the world (and very ufeful and moft refpectable men no doubt they are), who examine the pro's and the con's before they decide, upon the moft indifferent occafion; who are directed in all their actions by propriety, and by the general received notions of duty. They weigh, in the niceft fcales, every claim that an acquaintance, a relation, or a friend may have on them; and they endeavour to pay them on demand, as they would a bill of exchange. They calculate their income, and proportion every expence; and hearing it afferted every week in the moft folemn manner, that there is exceeding good intereft to be paid one time or other, for the money that is given to the poor, they rifk a little every year upon that venture. And their paffions, and their affairs are always in excellent order, and they walk through life undifturbed by the misfortunes of others. And when they come to the end of their journey, they are decently interred in a church-yard.

There is another fet of men, who never calculate; for they are generally guided by the heart, which never was taught arithmetic, and knows nothing of accounts. Their heads have fcarcely a vote in the choice of their acquaintances; and without the confent of the heart, moft certainly

certainly none in their friendſhips. They perform acts of benevolence, without recollecting that this is a duty, merely for the pleaſure they afford; and perhaps forget them, as they do their own pleaſures, when paſt.

As for little occaſional charities, theſe are as natural to ſuch characters as breathing; and they claim as little merit for the one as for the other, the whole ſeeming an affair of inſtinct rather than of reflection.

That the firſt of theſe two claſſes of men is the moſt uſeful in ſociety; that their affairs will be conducted with moſt circumſpection; that they will keep out of many ſcrapes and difficulties that the others may fall into; and that they are (if you inſiſt upon it very violently) the moſt virtuous of the two, I ſhall not diſpute:

difpute: Yet for the foul of me I cannot help preferring the other; for almoſt all the friends I have ever had in my life, are of the fecond claſs.

LETTER XVII.

Paris.

COnsidering the natural gaiety and volatility of the French nation, I have often been surprised at their fondness for tragedy, especially as their tragedies are barren of incident, full of long dialogues, and declamatory speeches;—and modelled according to the strictest code of critical legislation.

The most sprightly and fashionable people of both sexes flock to these entertainments in preference to all others, and listen with unrelaxed gravity and attention. One would imagine that such a serious, correct and uniform amusement, would be more congenial with the phlegm, and saturnine dispositions of the English, than with the gay, volatile temper of the French.

An Englifh audience loves fhow, buftle, and incident, in their tragedies; and have a mortal averfion to long dialogues and fpeeches, however fine the fentiments, and however beautiful the language may be.

In this it would feem, that the two nations had changed characters. Perhaps it would be difficult to account for it in a fatisfactory manner. I fhall not attempt it. A Frenchman would cut the matter fhort, by faying, that the Paris audience has a more correct and juft tafte than that of London; that the one could be amufed and delighted with poetry and fentiment, while the other could not be kept awake without buftle, guards, proceffions, trumpets, fighting, and murder.

For

For my own part, I admire the French Melpomene more in the clofet than on the ftage. I cannot be reconciled to the French actors of tragedy. Their pompous manner of declaiming feems to me very unnatural. The ftrut, and fuperb gef- tures, and what they call la manière noble, of their boafted Le Kain, appear, in my eyes, a little outrè.

The juftnefs, the dignified fimplicity, the energy of Garrick's action, have de- ftroyed my relifh for any manner different from his. That exquifite, but concealed art, that magic power, by which he could melt, freeze, terrify the foul, and com- mand the obedient paffions as he pleafed, we look for in vain, upon our own, or any other ftage.

What Horace faid of Nature, may be applied with equal juftice to that unri- valled actor:

———Juvat,

———————— Juvat, aut impellit ad iram,
Aut ad humum mœrore gravi deducit, et
angit.

One of the moſt difficult things in acting is the player's concealing himſelf behind the character he aſſumes: The inſtant the ſpectator gets a peep of him, the whole illuſion vaniſhes, and the pleaſure is ſucceeded by difguſt. In Oedipus, Mahomet, and Orofmane, I have always detected Le Kain; but I have ſeen the Engliſh Roſcius repreſent Hamlet, Lear, Richard, without recollecting that there was ſuch a perſon as David Garrick in the world.

The French tragedians are apt in my opinion *to overſtep the modeſty of nature:* Nature is not the criterion by which their merit is to be tried.—The audience meaſures them by a more ſublime ſtandard, and if they come not up to that, they cannot paſs muſter.

Natural

Natural action, and a natural elocution, they seem to think incompatible with dignity, and imagine that the hero must announce the greatness of his soul by supercilious looks, haughty gestures, and a hollow sounding voice. Such easy familiar dialogue as Hamlet holds with his old school-fellow Horatio, appears to them low, vulgar, and inconsistent with the dignity of tragedy.

But if simplicity of manners be not inconsistent, in real life, with genius, and the most exalted greatness of mind, I do not see why the actor who represents a hero, should always assume motions and gestures of uncommon dignity, and which we have no reason to think were ever in use in any age, or among any rank of men.

Simplicity of manners, however, is so far from being inconsistent with magnanimity, that the one for the most part accompanies

the

the other. The French have some reason to lean to this opinion; for two of the greatest men their nation ever produced were remarkable for the simplicity of their manners. Henry IV. and Maréchal Turenne were distinguished by that, as well as by their magnanimity and other heroic virtues.

How infinitely superior in real greatness and intrinsic merit, were those men to the strutting ostentatious Lewis, who was always affecting a greatness he never possessed,—till misfortune humbled his mind to the standard of humanity? Then indeed, throwing away his pageantry and bluster, he assumed true dignity, and for the first time obtained the admiration of the judicious. In the correspondence with de Torcy, Lewis's letters, which it is now certain were written and composed by himself, prove this, and display a soundness of judgement and real greatness of mind which seldom

dom appeared in the meridian of what they call his glory.

What Lewis was (in the height of his prosperity) to Henry in the essential qualities of a King and Hero, such is Le Kain to Garrick as an actor.

The French stage can boast at present of more than one actress who may dispute the laurel of tragedy with Mrs. Yates, or Mrs. Barry.

In comedy, the French actors excel, and can produce at all times a greater number far above mediocrity, than are to be found on the English stage.

The national character and manners of the French give them perhaps advantages in this line; and besides, they have more numerous resources to supply them with actors of every kind. In all the large

trading

trading and manufacturing towns, of which there are a great number in France, there are playhoufes eftablifhed. The fame thing takes place in moft of the frontier towns, and wherever there is a garrifon of two or three regiments.

There are companies of French comedians alfo at the northern courts, in all the large towns of Germany, and at fome of the courts in Italy. All of thefe are academies which educate actors for the Paris ftage.

In genteel comedy particularly, I imagine the French actors excel ours. They have in general more the appearance of people of fafhion.

There is not fuch a difference between the manners and behaviour of the people of the firft rank, and thofe of the middle and lower ranks, in France as in England.

Players

Players therefore, who wifh to catch the manners of people of high rank and fafhion, do not undertake fo great a tafk in the one country as in the other.

You very feldom meet with an Englifh fervant who could pafs for a man of quality or fafhion; and accordingly very few people who have been in that fituation ever appear on the Englifh ftage: But there are many *valets de place* in Paris fo very polite, fo completely poffeffed of all the little etiquettes, fafhionable phrafes, and ufual airs of the *beau monde*, that if they were fet off by the ornaments of drefs and equipage, they would pafs in many of the courts of Europe for men of fafhion, très polis,—bien aimables,—tout-à-fait comme il faut, et avec infiniment d'efprit; and could be detected only at the court of France, or by fuch foreigners as have had opportunities of obferving, and penetration to diftinguifh, the genuine cafe, and natural politenefs
Vol. I.   L   which

which prevail among the people of rank in this country.

In the character of a lively, petulant, genteel petit maitre of fashion, Mollé excels any actor in London.

The superiority of the French in genteel comedy is still more evident with regard to the actresses. Very few English actresses have appeared equal to the parts of Lady Betty Modish, in The Careless Husband, or of Millamant, in The Way of the World. Gross absurdity, extravagant folly and affectation are easily imitated; but the elegant coquetry, the lively, playful, agreeable affectation of these two finely imagined characters, require greater powers. I imagine, however, from the execution I have observed in similar parts, that there are several actresses on the French stage at present who could do them ample justice. Except Mrs. Barry and Mrs. Abington, I know no actress in England who could give an adequate idea of all that Congreve meant in Millamant.

It is remarkable, that the latter also excels in a character the moſt perfectly oppoſite to this, that of an ill taught, aukward, country girl. Perhaps there is no ſuch young lady in France as Congreve's Miſs Prue; but if there were many ſuch originals, no actreſs in that kingdom could give a copy more exquiſite than Mrs. Abington's.

In low comedy the French are delightful. I can form no notion of any thing ſuperior to Preville in many of his parts.

The little French operas which are given at the Comedie Italienne are executed in a much more agreeable manner than any thing of the ſame kind at London. Their balets alſo are more beautiful:—There is a gentilleſſe and legèreté in their manner of reprefenting thefe little fanciful pieces, which make our fingers and dancers appear fomewhat aukward and clumfy in the comparifon.

As for the Italian pieces, they are now performed only thrice a week, and the French feem to have loft in a great meafure their relifh for them. Carlin, the celebrated Harlequin, is the only fupport of thefe pieces. You are acquainted with the wonderful naïveté and comic powers of this man, which make us forget the extravagance of the Italian drama, and which can create objects of unbounded mirth, from a chaos of the moft incoherent and abfurd materials.

An advantageous figure, a graceful manner, a good voice, a ftrong memory, an accurate judgment, are all required in a player: Senfibility, and the power of expreffing the emotions of the heart by the voice and

and features, are indifpenfable. It feems therefore unreafonable, not to confider that profeffion as creditable, in which we expect fo many qualities united; while many others are thought refpectable, in which we daily fee people arrive at eminence without common fenfe.

This prejudice is ftill ftronger in France than in England. In a company where Monf. le Kain was, mention happened to be made, that the King of France had juft granted a penfion to a certain fuperannuated actor. An officer prefent, fixing his eyes on Le Kain, expreffed his indignation at fo much being beftowed on a rafcally player, while he himfelf had got nothing. Eh, Monfieur! retorted the actor, comptez-vous pour rien la liberté de me parler ainfi?

LETTER XVIII.

Geneva.

I Found myself so much hurried during the last week of my stay at Paris, that it was not in my power to write to you.

Ten thousand little affairs, which might have been arranged much better, and performed with more ease, had they been transacted as they occurred, were all crowded, by the slothful demon of procrastination, into the last bustling week, and executed in an imperfect manner.

I have often admired, without being able perfectly to imitate, those who have the happy talent of intermingling business with amusement.

Pleasure

Pleafure and bufinefs contraft and give a relifh to each other, like day and night, the conftant viciffitudes of which are far more delightful than an uninterrupted half year of either would be.

To pafs life in the moft agreeable manner, one ought not to be fo much a man of pleafure as to poftpone any neceffary bufinefs; nor fo much a man of bufinefs as to defpife elegant amufement. A proper mixture of both forms a more infallible fpecific againft *tedium* and fatigue, than a conftant regimen of the moft pleafant of the two.

As foon as I found the D—— of H—— difpofed to leave Paris, I made the neceffary arrangements for our departure, and a few days after we began our journey.

Paffing through Dijon, Chalons, Macon, and a country delightful to behold, but tedious

tedious to defcribe, we arrived on the fourth day at Lyons.

After Paris, Lyons is the moft magnificent town in France, enlivened by induftry, enriched by commerce, beautified by wealth, and by its fituation, in the middle of a fertile country, and at the confluence of the Saone and the Rhone. The numbers of inhabitants are eftimated at 200,000. The theatre is accounted the fineft in France, and all the luxuries in Paris are to be found at Lyons, though not in equal perfection.

The manners and converfation of merchants and manufacturers have been generally confidered as peculiar to themfelves. It is very certain that there is a ftriking difference in thefe particulars between the inhabitants of all the manufacturing and commercial towns of Britain, and thofe of Weftminfter. I could not remark the fame difference

difference between the manners and addrefs of the people of Lyons and the courtiers of Verfailles itfelf.

There appeared to me a wonderful fimilitude between the two. It is probable, however, that a Frenchman would perceive a difference where I could not. A foreigner does not obferve the different accents in which an Englifhman, a Scotchman, and an Irifhman fpeak Englifh; neither perhaps does he obferve any difference between the manners and addrefs of the inhabitants of Briftol, and thofe of Grofvenor-fquare, though all thefe are obvious to a native of England.

After a fhort ftay at Lyons, we proceeded to Geneva, and here we have remained thefe three weeks, without feeling the fmalleft inclination to fhift the fcene. That I fhould wifh to remain here is no way furprifing, but it was hardly to be expected

expected that the D— of H—— would have been of the same mind.—Fortunately, however, this is the case.—I know no place on the continent to which we could go with any probability of gaining by the change: The opportunities of improvement here are many, the amusements are few in number; and of a moderate kind: The hours glide along very smoothly, and though they are not always quickened by pleasure, they are unretarded by languor, and unruffled by remorse.

As for myself, I have been so very often and so miserably disappointed in my hopes of happiness by change, that I shall not, without some powerful motive, incline to forego my present state of content, for the chance of more exquisite enjoyments in a different place or situation.

I have at length learnt by my own experience (for not one in twenty profits by
the

the experience of others), that one great source of vexation proceeds from our indulging too sanguine hopes of enjoyment from the blessings we expect, and too much indifference for those we possess. We scorn a thousand sources of satisfaction which we might have had in the interim, and permit our comfort to be disturbed, and our time to pass unenjoyed, from impatience for some imagined pleasure at a distance, which we may perhaps never obtain, or which, when obtained, may change its nature, and be no longer pleasure. Young says,

> The present moment, like a wife, we shun,
> And ne'er enjoy, because it is our own.

The devil thus cheats men both out of the enjoyment of this life and of that which is to come, making us in the first place prefer the pleasures of this life to those of a future state, and then continually prefer
future

future pleasures in this life to these which are present.

The sum of all these apophthegms amounts to this:—We shall certainly remain at Geneva till we become more tired of it than at present.

LETTER XIX.

Geneva.

THE situation of Geneva is in many respects as happy as the heart of man could defire, or his imagination conceive. The Rhone, rushing out of the noblest lake in Europe, flows through the middle of the city, which is encircled by fertile fields, cultivated by the industry, and adorned by the riches and taste, of the inhabitants.

The long ridge of mountains called Mount Jura on the one side, with the Alps, the Glaciers of Savoy, and the snowy head of Mont Blanc on the other, serve as boundaries to the most charmingly variegated landscape that ever delighted the eye.

With

With thefe advantages in point of fituation, the citizens of Geneva enjoy freedom untainted by licentioufnefs, and fecurity unbought by the horrors of war.

The great number of men of letters, who either are natives of the place, or have chofen it for their refidence, the decent manners, the eafy circumftances, and humane difpofitions of the Genevois in general, render this city and its environs a very defirable retreat for people of a philofophic turn of mind, who are contented with moderate and calm enjoyments, have no local attachments or domeftic reafons for preferring another country, and who wifh in a certain degree to retire from the buftle of the world to a narrower and calmer fcene, and there for the reft of their days—

Ducere folicitæ jucunda oblivia vitæ.

As education here is equally cheap and liberal, the citizens of Geneva of both fexes
are

are remarkably well inſtructed. I do not imagine that any country in the world can produce an equal number of perſons (taken without election from all degrees and profeſſions) with minds ſo much cultivated as the inhabitants of Geneva poſſeſs.

It is not uncommon to find mechanics in the intervals of their labour amuſing themſelves with the works of Locke, Monteſquieu, Newton, and other productions of the ſame kind.

When I ſpeak of the cheapneſs of a liberal education, I mean for the natives and citizens only; for ſtrangers now find every thing dear at Geneva. Wherever Engliſhmen reſort, this is the caſe. If they do not find things dear, they ſoon make them ſo.

The democratical nature of their government inſpires every citizen with an idea of his own importance: He perceives

that

that no man in the republic can infult, or even neglect him, with impunity.

It is an excellent circumftance in any government, when the moft powerful man in the ftate has fomething to fear from the moft feeble. This is the cafe here: The meaneft citizen of Geneva is poffeffed of certain rights, which render him an object deferving the attention of the greateft. Befides, a confcioufnefs of this makes him refpect himfelf; a fentiment, which, within proper bounds, has a tendency to render a man refpectable to others.

The general character of human nature forbids us to expect that men will always act from motives of public fpirit, without an eye to private intereft. The beft form of government, therefore, is that in which the intereft of individuals is moft intimately blended with the public good.—This may be more perfectly accomplifhed in a
fmall

small republic than in a great monarchy.—In the first, men of genius and virtue are discovered and called to offices of truſt by the impartial admiration of their fellow-citizens;—in the other, the higheſt places are diſpoſed of by the caprice of the prince, or of his miſtreſs, or of thoſe courtiers, male or female, who are neareſt his perſon, watch the variations of his humour, and know how to ſeize the ſmiling moments, and turn them to their own advantage or that of their dependents. Monteſquieu ſays, that a ſenſe of honour produces the ſame effects in a monarchy, that public ſpirit or patriotiſm does in a republic: It muſt be remembered, however, that the firſt, according to the modern acceptation of the word, is generally confined to the nobility and gentry; whereas public ſpirit is a more univerſal principle, and ſpreads through all the members of the commonwealth.

VOL. I.   M   As

As far as I can judge, a spirit of independency and freedom, tempered by sentiments of decency and the love of order, influence, in a most remarkable manner, the minds of the subjects of this happy republic.

Before I knew them, I had formed an opinion, that the people of this place were fanatical, gloomy-minded, and unsociable, as the puritans in England, and the presbyterians in Scotland were, during the civil wars, and the reigns of Charles II. and his brother. In this, however, I find I had conceived a very erroneous notion.

There is not, I may venture to assert, a city in Europe where the minds of the people are less under the influence of superstition or fanatical enthusiasm than at Geneva. Servetus, were he now alive, would not run the smallest risk of persecution. The present clergy have, I am persuaded, as little the inclination as the power of molesting any person for speculative opinions. Should the Pope himself chuse this city for a retreat, it would be his own fault if he did not live in as much security as at the Vatican.

The clergy of Geneva in general are men of sense, learning, and moderation, impressing upon the minds of their hearers the tenets of Christianity with all the graces of pulpit eloquence, and illustrating the efficacy of the doctrine by their conduct in life.

The people of every station in this place attend sermons and the public worship with remarkable punctuality. The Sunday is honoured with the most respectful decorum during the hours of divine service; but as soon as that is over, all the usual amusements commence.

The public walks are crowded by all degrees of people in their beſt dreſſes.—The different ſocieties, and what they call circles, aſſemble in the houſes and gardens of individuals.—They play at cards and at bowls, and have parties upon the lake with muſic.

There is one cuſtom univerſal here, and, as far as I know, peculiar to this place: The parents form ſocieties for their children at a very early period of their lives. Theſe ſocieties conſiſt of ten, a dozen, or more children of the ſame ſex, and nearly of the ſame age and ſituation in life. They aſſemble once a week in the houſes of the different parents, who entertain the company by turns with tea, coffee, biſcuits and fruit; and then leave the young aſſembly to the freedom of their own converſation.

This connection is ſtrictly kept up through life, whatever alterations may take place

place in the situations or circumstances of the individuals. And although they should afterwards form new or preferable intimacies, they never entirely abandon this society; but to the latest period of their lives continue to pass a few evenings every year with the companions of their youth and their earliest friends.

The richer class of the citizens have country-houses adjacent to the town, where they pass one half of the year. These houses are all of them neat, and some of them splendid. One piece of magnificence they possess in greater perfection than the most superb villa of the greatest lord in any other part of the world can boast, I mean the prospect which almost all of them command.—The gardens and vineyards of the republic,—the Païs de Vaux;—Geneva with its lake;—innumerable country-seats;—castles, and little towns around the lake;—the vallies of Savoy, and the loftiest
moun-

mountains of the Alps, all within one sweep of the eye.

Those whose fortunes or employments do not permit them to pass the summer in the country, make frequent parties of pleasure upon the lake, and dine and spend the evening at some of the villages in the environs, where they amuse themselves with music and dancing.

Sometimes they form themselves into circles consisting of forty or fifty persons, and purchase or hire a house and garden near the town, where they assemble every afternoon during the summer, drink coffee, lemonade, and other refreshing liquors; and amuse themselves with cards, conversation, and playing at bowls; a game very different from that which goes by the same name in England; for here, instead of a smooth level green, they often chuse the roughest and most unequal piece of ground.

ground. The player, inftead of rolling the bowl, throws it in fuch a manner, that it refts in the place where it firft touches the ground; and if that be a fortunate fituation, the next player pitches his bowl directly on his adverfary's, fo as to make that fpring away, while his own fixes itfelf in the fpot from which the other has been diflodged.— Some of the citizens are aftonifhingly dexterous at this game, which is more complicated and interefting than the Englifh manner of playing.

They generally continue thefe circles till the dufk of the evening, and the found of the drum from the ramparts call them to the town; and at that time the gates are fhut, after which no perfon can enter or go out, the officer of the guard not having the power to open them, without an order from the Syndics, which is not to be obtained but on fome great emergency.

LETTER XX.

Geneva.

THE mildnefs of the climate, the fublime beauties of the country, and the agreeable manners of the inhabitants, are not, in my opinion, the greateft attractions of this place.

Upon the fame hill, in the neighbourhood of Geneva, three Englifh families at prefent refide, whofe fociety would render any country agreeable.

The houfe of Mr. N—— is a temple of hofpitality, good humour, and friendfhip.

Near to him lives your acquaintance Mr. U——. He perfectly anfwers your defcription, lively, fenfible, and obliging;

and, I imagine, happier than ever you faw him, having fince that time drawn a great prize in the matrimonial lottery.

Their neareft neighbours are the family of Mr. L———. This gentleman, his lady and children, form one of the moft pleafing pictures of domeftic felicity I ever beheld. He himfelf is a man of refined tafte, a benevolent mind, and elegant manners.

Thefe three families, who live in the greateft cordiality with the citizens of Geneva, their own countrymen, and one another, render the hill of Cologny the moft delightful place perhaps at this moment in the world.

The Englifh gentlemen, who refide in the town, often refort hither, and mix with parties of the beft company of Geneva.

I am

I am told, that our young countrymen never were on so friendly and sociable a footing with the citizens of this republic as at present, owing in a great degree to the conciliatory manners of these three families, and to the great popularity of an English nobleman, who has lived with his lady and son in this state for several years.

I formerly mentioned, that all who live in town, must return from their visits in the country at sun-set, otherwise they are certain of being shut out;—the Genevois being wonderfully jealous of the external, as well as the internal enemies of their independency. This jealousy has been transmitted from one generation to another, ever since the attempt made by the Duke of Savoy, in the year 1602, to seize upon the town.

He marched an army, in the middle of a dark night, in the time of peace, to the gates,

gates, applied fcaling ladders to the ramparts and walls, and having furprifed the centinels, feveral hundreds of the Savoyard foldiers had actually got into the town, and the reft were following, when they were at length difcovered by a woman, who gave the alarm.

The Genevois ftarted from their fleep, feized the readieft arms they could find, attacked the affailants with fpirit and energy, killed numbers in the ftreet, drove others out of the gate, or tumbled them over the ramparts, and the few who were taken prifoners, they beheaded next morning, without further procefs or ceremony.

The Genevois annually diftinguifh the day on which this memorable exploit was performed, as a day of public thankfgiving and rejoicing.

It

It is called le jour de l'Efcalade. There is divine worſhip in all the churches.——The clergymen, on this occaſion, after ſermon, recapitulate all the circumſtances of this intereſting event; put the audience in mind of the gratitude they owe to Divine Providence, and to the valour of their anceſtors, which ſaved them in ſo remarkable a manner from civil and religious bondage; enumerate the peculiar bleſſings which they enjoy, and exhort them, in the moſt pathetic ſtrain, to watch over their liberties, remain ſteady in their religion, and tranſmit theſe, and all their other advantages, unimpaired to their poſterity.

The evening of the jour de l'Efcalade is ſpent in viſiting, feaſting, dancing, and all kinds of diverſions; for the Genevois ſeldom venture on great feſtivity, till they have previouſly performed their religious duties——In this, obſerving the maxim
of

of the Pſalmiſt,—to join trembling with their mirth.

The State keeps in pay a garriſon of ſix hundred mercenaries, who mount guard and do duty every day. But they do not truſt the ſafety of the republic to theſe alone. All citizens of Geneva are ſoldiers. They are exerciſed ſeveral hours, daily, for two months, every ſummer; during which time they wear their uniforms, and at the end of that period are reviewed by the Syndics.

As they receive no pay, and as the officers are their fellow-citizens, it cannot be imagined that theſe troops will perform the manual exerciſe and military evolutions, with the exactneſs of ſoldiers who have no other occupation, and who are under all the rigour of military diſcipline.

Never-

Neverthelefs they make a very refpectable figure in the eyes even of difinterefted fpectators; who are, however, but few in number, the greater part confifting of their own parents, wives and children. So, I dare fwear, there are no troops in the world, who, at a review, are beheld with more approbation than thofe of Geneva.

Even a ftranger of a moderate fhare of fenfibility, who recollects the connection between the troops and the beholders, who obferves the anxiety, the tendernefs, the exultation, and various movements of the heart, which appear in the countenances of the fpectators, will find it difficult to remain unconcerned:——But fympathifing with all around him, he will naturally yield to the pleafing emotions, and at length behold the militia of Geneva with the eyes of a citizen of the republic.

Geneva,

Geneva, like all free states, is exposed to party-rage, and the public harmony is frequently interrupted by political squabbles. Without entering into a detail of the particular disputes which agitate them at present, I shall tell you in general, that one part of the citizens are accused of a design of throwing all the power into the hands of a few families, and of establishing a complete aristocracy. The other opposes every measure which is supposed to have that tendency, and by their adversaries are accused of seditious designs.

It is difficult for strangers who reside here any considerable time, to observe a strict neutrality. The English in particular are exceedingly disposed to take part with one side or other; and as the government has not hitherto attempted to bribe them, they generally attach themselves to the opposition.

Walking

Walking one afternoon with a young nobleman, who, to a ſtrong taſte for natural philoſophy, unites the moſt paſſionate zeal for civil liberty, we paſſed near the garden, in which one of thoſe circles which ſupport the pretenſions of the magiſtracy aſſemble. I propoſed joining them. No, ſaid my Lord, with indignation; I will not go for a moment into ſuch a ſociety: I conſider theſe men as the enemies of their country, and that place as a focus for conſuming freedom.

Among the citizens themſelves, political altercations are carried on with great fire and ſpirit. A very worthy old gentleman, in whoſe houſe I have been often entertained with great hoſpitality, declaiming warmly againſt certain meaſures of the council, aſſerted, that all thoſe who had promoted them deſerved death; and if it depended on him, they ſhould all be hanged, without loſs of time. His brother, who was in that predicament, interrupted him, and said, with a tone of voice which seemed to beg for mercy, Good God! brother! surely you would not push your resentment so far: you would not actually hang them? Oui assurement, replied the patriot, with a determined countenance, et vous, mon très cher frere, vous seriez le premier pendu pour montrer mon impartialité.

LETTER XXI.

Geneva.

ALTHOUGH this republic has long continued in a profound peace, and there is no great probability of its being soon engaged in bloody conflict, yet the citizens of Geneva are not the less fond of the pomp of war.

This appears in what they call their military feasts, which are their most favourite amusements, and which they take every opportunity of enjoying.

I was present lately at a very grand entertainment of this kind, which was given by the King of the Arquebusiers upon his accession to the royal dignity.

This envied rank is neither tranfmitted by hereditary right, nor obtained by election; but gained by fkill and real merit.

A war with this ftate, like the war of Troy, muft neceffarily confift of a fiege. The fkilful ufe of the cannon and arquebufe is therefore thought to be of the greateft importance. During feveral months every year, a confiderable number of the citizens are almoft conftantly employed in firing at a mark, which is placed at a proper diftance.

Any citizen has a right, at a fmall expence, to make trial of his fkill in this way; and after a due number of trials, the moft expert markfman is declared King.

There has not been a coronation of this kind thefe ten years, his late Majefty having kept peaceable poffeffion of the throne

during

during that period. But this summer, Mr. Moses Maudrier was found to excel in skill every competitor; and was raised to the throne by the unanimous voice of the judges.

He was attended to his own house from the field of contest by the Syndics, amidst the acclamations of the people. Some time after this, on the day of his feast, a camp was formed on a plain, without the gates of the city.

Here the whole forces of the republic, both horse and foot, were assembled, and divided into two distinct armies. They were to perform a battle in honour of his Majesty, all the combatants having previously studied their parts.

This very ingenious, warlike drama had been composed by one of the reverend ministers, minifters, who is faid to poffefs a very extenfive military genius.

That the ladies and people of diftinction, who were not to be actually engaged, might view the action with the greater eafe and fafety, a large amphitheatre of feats was prepared for them, at a convenient diftance from the field of battle.

Every thing being in readinefs, the Syndics, the Council, ftrangers of diftinction, and the relations and favourites of the King, affembled at his Majefty's palace, which is a little fnug houfe, fituated in a narrow lane in the lower part of the city. From the palace, the proceffion fet out in the following order:

His Majefty walked firft, fupported by the two oldeft Syndics.

In the next rank was the Duke of H——, with the youngeſt.

After theſe, walked Lord St——pe, the Prince Gallitzen,—Mr. Cl—ve, ſon to Lord Cl—ve; Mr. Gr—lle, ſon to the late Miniſter; Mr. St. L——, and many other Engliſh gentlemen, who had been invited to the feaſt.

Next to them came the Council of twenty-five; and the proceſſion was cloſed by the King's particular friends and relations.

In this order they marched through the city, preceded by a band of muſic, who played, as you may believe, the moſt martial tunes they poſſibly could think of.

When this company came to the field where the troops were drawn up, they were

were faluted by the officers; and having made a complete circuit of both armies, the King and all his attendants took their feats at the amphitheatre, which had been prepared for that purpofe.

The impatience of the troops had been very vifible for fome time. When the King was feated, their ardour could be no longer reftrained. They called loudly to their officers to lead them to glory.——— The fignal was given.—They advanced to the attack in the moft undaunted manner.———Confcious that they fought under the eyes of their King, the Syndics, of their wives, children, mothers and grandmothers, they difdained the thoughts of retreat.———They ftood undifturbed by the thickeft fire. They fmiled at the roaring of the cannon, and like the horfe in Job, they cried among the trumpets, ha, ha!

The ingenious author of the battle had taken care to diverſify it with ſeveral entertaining incidents.

An ambuſcade was placed by one of the armies, behind ſome trees, to ſurpriſe the enemy.——This ſucceeded to a miracle, although the ambuſcade was poſted in the ſight of both armies, and all the ſpectators.

A convoy with proviſions, advancing towards one of the armies, was attacked by a detachment from the other; and after a ſmart ſkirmiſh, one half of the waggons were carried away by the aſſailants :—The other remained with the troops for whom they ſeemed to have been originally intended.

A wooden bridge was briſkly attacked, and as reſolutely defended; but at length was trod to pieces by both armies; for, in the fury of the fight, the combatants forgot

got whether this poor bridge was their friend or their foe. By what means it got into the midſt of the battle, I never could conceive; for there was neither river, brook, nor ditch in the whole field.

The cavalry on both ſides performed wonders.——It was difficult to determine which of the generals diſtinguiſhed himſelf moſt. They were both dreſſed in clothes exuberantly covered with lace; for the ſumptuary laws were ſuſpended for this day, that the battle might be as magnificent as poſſible.

As neither of theſe gallant commanders would conſent to the being defeated, the reverend author of the engagement could not make the cataſtrophe ſo deciſive and affecting as he intended.

While Victory, with equipoiſed wings, hovered over both armies, a meſſenger arrived

rived from the town-hall with intelligence that dinner was ready. This news quickly spread among the combatants, and had an effect similar to that which the Sabine women produced when they rushed between their ravishers and their relations.—The warriors of Geneva relented at once; and both armies suspended their animosity, in the contemplation of that which they both loved.——They threw down their arms, shook hands, and were friends.

Thus ended the battle.——I don't know how it will affect you; but it has fatigued me so completely, that I have lost all appetite for the feast, which must therefore be delayed till another post.

LETTER XXII.

Geneva.

THE fame company which had attended the King to the field of battle, marched with him in proceſſion from that to the Maiſon de Ville, where a ſumptuous entertainment was prepared.

This was exactly the reverſe of a fête champetre, being held in the town-houſe, and in the middle of the ſtreets adjacent; where tables were covered, and dinner provided, for ſeveral hundreds of the officers and ſoldiers.

The King, the Syndics, moſt of the members of the Council, and all the ſtrangers, dined in the town-hall. The other rooms,

rooms, as well as the outer court, were likewife full of company.

There was much greater havoc at dinner than had been at the battle, and the entertainment in other refpects was nearly as warlike.

A kettle-drum was placed in the middle of the hall, upon which a martial flourifh was performed at every toaft. This was immediately anfwered by the drums and trumpets without the hall, and the cannon of the baftion.

Profperity to the republic is a favourite toaft:—When this was announced by the firft Syndic, all the company ftood up with their fwords drawn in one hand, and glaffes filled with wine in the other.

· Having drank the toaft, they clafhed their fwords, a ceremony always performed in every circle or club where there is a public

lic dinner, as often as this particular toaſt is named.——It is an old cuſtom, and implies that every man is ready to fight in defence of the republic.

After we had been about two hours at table, a new ceremony took place, which I expected as little in the middle of a feaſt. An hundred grenadiers, with their ſwords drawn, marched with great ſolemnity into the middle of the hall, for the tables being placed in the form of a horſe-ſhoe, there was vacant ſpace in the middle ſufficient to admit them.

They deſired permiſſion to give a toaſt: This being granted, each of the granadiers, by a well-timed movement, like a motion in the exerciſe, pulled from his pocket a large water-glaſs, which being immediately filled with wine, one of the ſoldiers, in the name of all, drank a health to King Moſes the firſt. His example was followed by his
compa-

companions and all the company, and was inftantly honoured by the found of the drums, trumpets, and artillery.

When the grenadiers had drank this, and a toaft or two more, they wheeled about, and marched out of the hall with the fame folemnity with which they had entered, refuming their places at the tables in the ftreet.

Soon after this a man fantaftically dreffed entered the hall, and diftributed among the company fome printed fheets which feemed to have come directly from the prefs.

This proved to be a fong made for the occafion, replete with gaiety, wit, and good fenfe, pointing out, in a humorous ftrain, the advantages which the citizens of Geneva poffeffed, and exhorting them to unanimity, induftry, and public fpirit.—This ditty was fung by the man who brought it,
while

while many of the company joined in the chorus.

When we defcended from the town-hall, we found the foldiers intermingled with their officers, ftill feated at the tables in the ftreets, and encircled by their wives and children.

They all arofe foon after, and dividing into different companies, repaired to the ramparts, the fields, and the gardens, where, with mufic and dancing, they continued in high glee during the reft of the evening.

The whole exhibition of the day, though no very juft reprefentation of the manœuvres of war, or the elegance of a court entertainment, formed the moft lively picture of jollity, mirth, good-humour and cordiality, that I had ever feen.

The

The inhabitants of a whole city,—of a whole ſtate if you pleaſe, united in one ſcene of good fellowſhip, like a ſingle family, is ſurely no common ſight.

If this ſketch conveys one half of the ſatisfaction to your mind, which the ſcene itſelf afforded mine, you will not think theſe two long letters tedious.

LETTER XXIII.

Geneva.

THERE are some of the citizens of Geneva themselves who deride the little military establishment of the republic, and declare it to be highly ridiculous in such a feeble state to presume that they could defend themselves. The very idea of resistance against Savoy or France, they hold as absurd.

They seem to take pleasure in mortifying their countrymen, assuring them, that in case of an attack all their efforts would be fruitless, and their garrison unable to stand a siege of ten days.

These politicians declaim against the needless expence of keeping the fortifications in repair, and they calculate the money loft, by fo many manufacturers being employed in wielding ufelefs firelocks, inftead of the tools of their refpective profeffions.

Were I a member of this republic, I fhould have no patience with thefe difcouraging malcontents, who endeavour to deprefs the minds of their countrymen, and embitter a fource of real enjoyment.

I am convinced that the garrifon, fmall as it is, aided by the zeal of the inhabitants, and regulated by that fhare of difcipline which their fituation admits, would be fufficient to fecure them from a coup-de-main, or any immediate infult, and might enable them to defend the town from the attempts of any one of the neighbouring ftates, till they fhould receive fuccour from fome of the others.

Inde-

Independent of thefe confiderations, the ramparts are moft agreeable walks, convenient for the inhabitants, and ornamental to the city.

The exercifing and reviewing the militia form an innocent and agreeable fpectacle to the women and children, contribute to the health and amufement of the troops themfelves, infpire the inhabitants in general with the pleafing ideas of fecurity and of their own importance.

Upon the whole, I am convinced that the fortifications, and the militia of Geneva, produce more happinefs, in thefe various ways taken together, than could be purchafed by all the money they coft, expended in any other manner.

This I imagine is more than can be faid in favour of the greater part of the ftanding armies on the continent of Europe, whose numbers secure the despotism of the prince, whose maintenance is a most severe burthen upon the countries which support them, and whose discipline, instead of exciting pleasing emotions, impresses the mind with horror.

The individuals who compose those armies are miserable, by the tyranny exercised on them, and are themselves the cause of misery to their fellow-citizens by the tyranny they exercise.

But it will be said they defend the nation from foreign enemies.—Alas, could a foreign conqueror occasion more wretchedness than such defenders?———When he who calls himself my protector has stripped me of my property, and deprived me of my freedom, I cannot return him very cordial thanks, when he tells me, that he will defend me from every other robber.

The

The moſt ſolid ſecurity which this little republic has for its independency, is founded on the mutual jealouſy of its neighbours.

There is no danger of its meeting with the misfortune which has ſo lately befallen Poland.—Geneva is ſuch an atom of a ſtate as not to be diviſible.

It ſerves, however, as a kind of barrier or alarm-poſt to the Swiſs Cantons, particularly that of Bern, which certainly would not like to ſee it in the hands either of the King of France or of Sardinia.

The acquiſition is not worth the attention of the firſt; and it is better for the ſecond, that the republic ſhould remain in its preſent free and independent ſituation, than that it ſhould revert to his poſſeſſion, and be ſubjected to the ſame government with his other dominions.

For no fooner would Geneva be in the poffeffion of Sardinia, than the wealthieft of the citizens would abandon it, and carry their families and riches to Switzerland, Holland, or England.

Trade and manufactures would dwindle with the fpirit and independence of the inhabitants; and the flourifhing, enlightened, happy city of Geneva, like other towns of Piedmont and Savoy, would become the refidence of oppreffion, fuperftition, and poverty.

In this fituation it could add but little to the King's revenue; whereas, at prefent, the peafants of his dominions refort in great numbers to Geneva every market-day, where they find a ready fale for all the productions of their farms. The land is, on this account, more valuable, and the peafants are more at their eafe, though the taxes are very high, than in any other part of Savoy.

This

This republic, therefore, in its prefent independent ftate, is of more ufe to the King of Sardinia, than if it were his property.

If a wealthy merchant fhould purchafe a piece of ground from a poor Lord, build a large houfe, and form beautiful gardens upon it, keep a number of fervants, fpend a great part of his revenue in good houfe-keeping and hofpitality, the confumption of his table, and many other articles, being purchafed from this Lord's tenants, it is evident that they would become rich, and be able to pay a larger rent to their landlord. This Lord would certainly act againft his own intereft, if he attempted, by law, chicane, or force, to difpoffefs the proprietor of the houfe and gardens.

The free republic of Geneva is to the King of Sardinia, exactly what the fuppofed rich man would be to the poor Lord.

It affords me satisfaction to perceive, that the ſtability of this little fabric of freedom, raiſed by my friends the citizens of Geneva, does not depend on the juſtice and moderation of the neighbouring powers, or any equivocal ſupport; but is founded on the ſolid, laſting pillars of their mutual intereſt.

LETTER XXIV.

Geneva.

I Returned a few days since from a journey to the Glaciers of Savoy, the Pays de Vallais, and other places among the Alps.

The wonderful accounts I had heard of the Glaciers had excited my curiosity a good deal, while the air of superiority assumed by some who had made this boasted tour, piqued my pride still more.

One could hardly mention any thing curious or singular, without being told by some of those travellers, with an air of cool contempt—Dear Sir,—that is pretty well; but, take my word for it, it is nothing to the Glaciers of Savoy.

I deter-

I determined at laſt not to take their word for it, and I found ſome gentlemen of the ſame way of thinking. The party conſiſted of the Duke of H——, Mr. U—, Mr. G——, Mr. K——, and myſelf.

We left Geneva early in the morning of the third of Auguſt, and breakfaſted at Bonneville, a ſmall town in the duchy of Savoy, ſituated at the foot of Mole, and on the banks of the river Arve.

The ſummit of Mole, as we were told, is about 4600 Engliſh feet above the lake of Geneva, at the lower paſſage of the Rhone, which laſt is about 1200 feet above the level of the Mediterranean. For theſe particulars, I ſhall take the word of my informer, whatever airs of ſuperiority he may aſſume on the diſcovery.

From Bonneville we proceeded to Cluſe, by a road tolerably good, and highly en-
                                            tertaining

tertaining on account of the fingularity and variety of landfcape to be feen from it. The objects change their appearance every moment as you advance, for the path is continually winding, to humour the pofition of the mountains, and to gain an accefs between the rocks, which in fome places hang over it in a very threatening manner. The mountains overlook and prefs fo clofely upon this little town of Clufe, that when I ftood in the principal ftreet, each end of it feemed to be perfectly fhut up; and wherever any of the houfes had fallen down, the vacancy appeared to the eye, at a moderate diftance, to be plugged up in the fame manner by a green mountain.

On leaving Clufe, however, we found a well-made road running along the banks of the Arve, and flanked on each fide by very high hills, whofe oppofite fides tally fo exactly, as to lead one to imagine they have

been

been torn from each other by some violent convulsion of nature.

In other places one side of this defile is a high perpendicular rock, so very smooth that it seems not to have been torn by nature, but chifelled by art, from top to bottom, while the whole of the side directly opposite is of the most smiling verdure.

The passage between the mountains gradually opens as you advance, and the scene diversifies with a fine luxuriancy of wild landscape.

Before you enter the town of Sallenche, you must cross the Arve, which at this season is much larger than in winter, being swelled by the dissolving snows of the Alps.

This river has its source at the Parish of Argentiere, in the valley of Chamouni, is

imme-

immediately augmented by torrents from the neighbouring Glaciers, and pours its chill turbid ſtream into the Rhone, ſoon after that river iſſues from the lake of Geneva.

The contraſt between thoſe two rivers is very ſtriking, the one being as pure and limpid as the other is foul and muddy. The Rhone ſeems to ſcorn the alliance, and keeps as long as poſſible unmingled with his dirty ſpouſe. Two miles below the place of their junction, a difference and oppoſition between this ill-ſorted couple is ſtill obſervable; theſe, however, gradually abate by long habit, till at laſt, yielding to neceſſity, and to thoſe unrelenting laws which joined them together, they mix in perfect union, and flow in a common ſtream to the end of their courſe.

We

We paffed the night at Sallenche, and the remaining part of our journey not admitting of chaifes, they were fent back to Geneva, with orders to the drivers, to go round by the other fide of the lake, and meet us at the village of Martigny, in the Pays de Vallais.

We agreed with a muleteer at Sallenche, who provided mules to carry us over the mountains to Martigny. It is a good day's journey from Sallenche to Chamouni, not on account of the diftance, but from the difficulty and perplexity of the road, and the fteep afcents and defcents with which you are teafed alternately the whole way.

Some of the mountains are covered with pine, oak, beech, and walnut trees. Thefe are interfperfed with apple, plum, cherry, and other fruit trees, fo that we rode a great part of the forenoon in fhade.

Befides

Besides the refreshing coolness this occasioned, it was most agreeable to me on another account. The road was in some places so exceedingly steep, that I never doubted but some of us were to fall; I therefore reflected with satisfaction, that those trees would probably arrest our course, and hinder us from rolling a great way.

But many pathless craggy mountains remained to be traversed after we had lost the protection of the trees. We then had nothing but the sagacity of our mules to trust to. For my own part, I was very soon convinced that it was much safer on all dubious occasions to depend on their's than on my own: For as often as I was presented with a choice of difficulties, and the mule and I were of different opinions, if, becoming more obstinate than he, I insisted on his taking my track, I never failed to repent it, and often was obliged to return to the place where the controversy had

begun,

begun, and follow the path to which he had pointed at firſt.

It is entertaining to obſerve the prudence of theſe animals in making their way down ſuch dangerous rocks. They ſometimes put their heads over the edge of the precipice, and examine with anxious circumſpection every poſſible way by which they can deſcend, and at length are ſure to fix on that which upon the whole is the beſt. Having obſerved this in ſeveral inſtances, I laid the bridle on the neck of my mule, and allowed him to take his own way, without preſuming to controul him in the ſmalleſt degree.

This is doubtleſs the beſt method, and what I recommend to all my friends in their journey through life, when they have mules for their companions.

We

We rested some time, during the sultry heat of the day, at a very pleasingly situated village called Serve; and ascending thence along the steepest and roughest road we had yet seen, we passed by a mountain, wherein, they told us, there is a rich vein of copper, but that the proprietors have left off working it for many years.

As we passed through one little village, I saw many peasants going into a church.—It was some Saint's day.——The poor people must have half-ruined themselves by purchasing gold-leaf.—Every thing was gilded.—The virgin was dressed in a new gown of gold-paper;——the infant in her arms was equally brilliant, all but the periwig on his head, which was milk-white, and had certainly been fresh powdered that very morning.

I could scarcely refrain from smiling at this ridiculous sight, which the people beheld with as much veneration as they could have shewn, had the originals been prefent.

Upon cafting up my eyes to the cieling, I faw fomething more extraordinary ftill: This was a portrait of God the Father, fitting on a cloud, and dreffed like a Pope, with the tiara on his head. Any one muft naturally be fhocked at this, if he be not at the fame inftant moved to laughter at the infinite abfurdity of the idea.

About fix in the evening we arrived at the valley of Chamouni, and found lodgings in a fmall village called Prieuré. The valley of Chamouni is about fix leagues in length, and an Englifh mile in breadth. It is bounded on all fides by very high mountains. Between the intervals of thefe mountains, on one fide of the valley, the vaft bodies of fnow and ice, which are called Glaciers, defcend from mount Blanc, which is their fource.

On

On one side of the valley, oppofite to the Glaciers, ſtands Breven, a mountain whoſe ridge is 5300 Engliſh feet higher than the valley. Many travellers who have more curioſity, and who think leſs of fatigue than we, take their firſt view of the Glaciers from the top of mount Breven. As there is only the narrow valley between that and the Glaciers, all of which it overlooks, and every other object around, except Mont Blanc, the view from it muſt be very advantageous and magnificent.

We determined to begin with Montanvert, from which we could walk to the Glaciers, reſerving Mount Breven for another day's work, if we ſhould find ourſelves ſo inclined. After an hour's refreſhment at our quarters, Mr. K—— and I took a walk through the valley.

The chapter of Prieſts and Canons of Sallenche have the lordſhip of Chamouni, and draw a revenue from the poor inhabitants; the higheſt mountains of the Alps, with all their ice and ſnow, not being ſufficient to defend them from rapacity and extortion.

The prieſt's houſe is beyond compariſon the beſt in the whole valley. Looking at it, I aſked a young man who ſtood near me, if the prieſt was rich?

Oui, Monſieur, horriblement,—replied he,—et auſſi il mange preſque tout notre blé?

I then aſked, if the people of Chamouni wiſhed to get rid of him?

Oui, bien de celui-ci—mais il faut avoir un autre.

I do not ſee the abſolute neceſſity of that, ſaid I.——Conſider, if you had no prieſt, you would have more to eat.

The

The lad ſtared——then anſwered with great *naiveté*—Ah, Monſieur, dans ce pays-ci les prêtres ſont tout auſſi neceſſaires que le manger.

It is plain, that this clergyman inſtructs his pariſhioners very carefully in the principles of religion.——I perceive, that your ſoul is in very ſafe hands, ſaid K——, giving the boy a crown; but here is ſomething to enable you to take care of your body.

In my next I ſhall endeavour to give you ſome account of the Glaciers:—At preſent, I muſt wiſh you good night.

LETTER XXV.

Geneva.

WE began pretty early in the morning to afcend Montanvert, from the top of which, there is eafy accefs to the Glacier of that name, and to the valley of ice.

Our mules carried us from the inn acrofs the valley, and even for a confiderable way up the mountain; which at length became fo exceedingly fteep, that we were obliged to difmount and fend them back. Mr. U—— only, who had been here before, and was accuftomed to fuch expeditions, continued without compunction on his mule till he got to the top, riding fearlefs over rocks, which a goat or a chamois would have paffed with caution.

In

In this laſt animal, which is to be found on theſe mountains only, are blended the different qualities of the goat and the deer.——It is ſaid to have more agility than any other quadruped poſſeſſed of the ſame degree of ſtrength.

After aſcending four hours, we gained the ſummit of Montanvert. The day was remarkably fine, the objects around noble and majeſtic, but in ſome reſpects different from what I had expected.

The valley of Chamouni had diſappeared:—Mount Breven ſeemed to have crept wonderfully near; and if I had not juſt croſſed the plain which ſeparates the two mountains, and is a mile in breadth, I ſhould have concluded that their baſes were in contact, and that their diſtance above was ſolely owing to the diminution in the ſize of all mountains towards the ſummit. Judging from the eye alone, I
ſhould

fhould have thought it poffible to have thrown a ftone from the place where I ftood to Mount Breven.

There is a chain of mountains behind Montanvert, all covered with fnow, which terminate in four diftinct rocks, of a great height, having the appearance of narrow pyramids or fpires. They are called the Needles; and each has a diftinct name.—Mont Blanc, furrounded by Montanvert, Mount Breven, the Needles, and other fnowy mountains, appears like a giant among pygmies.

The height which we had now attained, was fo far on our way up this mountain. I was therefore equally furprifed and mortified to find, after an afcent of three thoufand feet, that Mont Blanc feemed as high here as when we were in the valley.

Having

Having afcended Montanvert from Chamouni, on defcending a little on the other fide, we found ourfelves on a plain, whofe appearance has been aptly compared to that which a ſtormy fea would have, if it were fuddenly arrefted and fixed by a ftrong froft. This is called the Valley of Ice. It ftretches feveral leagues behind Montanvert, and is reckoned 2300 feet higher than the valley of Chamouni.

From the higheft part of Montanvert we had all the following objects under our eye, fome of which feemed to obſtruct the view of others equally interefting;——the Valley of Ice, the Needles, Mont Blanc, with the fnowy mountains below, finely contrafted with Breven, and the green hills on the oppofite fide of Chamouni, and the fun in full fplendor fhowing all of them to the greateft advantage.—The whole forms a fcene equally fublime and beautiful, far above my power of defcription,

and

and worthy of the eloquence of that very ingenious gentleman, who has so finely illustrated these subjects, in a particular treatise, and given so many examples of both in his parliamentary speeches.

While we remained in contemplation of this scene, some of the company observed, that from the top of one of the Needles the prospect would be still more magnificent, as the eye could stretch over Breven, beyond Geneva, all the way to Mount Jura, and comprehend the Pays de Vallais, and many other mountains and vallies.

This excited the ambition of the D— of H—. He sprung up, and made towards the Aiguille du Dru, which is the highest of the four Needles. Though he bounded over the ice with the elasticity of a young chamois, it was a considerable time before he could arrive at the foot of the Needle:—

for

for people are greatly deceived as to diſtances, in thoſe ſnowy regions.

Should he get near the top, ſaid Mr. G——, looking after him with eagerneſs, he will ſwear we have ſeen nothing—But, I will try to mount as high as he can;— I am not fond of ſeeing people above me. So ſaying, he ſprung after him.

In a ſhort time we ſaw them both ſcrambling up the rock:———The D—— had gained a conſiderable height, when he was ſuddenly ſtopped by a part of the rock which was perfectly impracticable (for his impetuoſity had prevented him from chooſing the eaſieſt way); ſo Mr. G—— overtook him.

Here they had time to breathe and cool a little. The one being determined not to be ſurpaſſed, the other thought the exploit

ploit not worth his while, fince the honour muft be divided. So like two rival powers, who have exhaufted their ftrength by a fruitlefs conteft, they returned, fatigued and difappointed, to the place from which they had fet out.

After a very agreeable repaft, on the provifions and wine which our guides had brought from the Prieuré, we paffed, by an eafy defcent, from the green part of Montanvert to the Valley of Ice. A walk upon this frozen fea is attended with inconveniencies. In fome places, the fwellings, which have been compared to waves, are forty or fifty feet high: yet, as they are rough, and the ice intermingled with fnow, one may walk over them. In other parts, thofe waves are of a very moderate fize, and in fome places the furface is quite level.

What

What renders a paſſage over this valley ſtill more difficult and dangerous is, the rents in the ice, which are to be met with, whatever direction you follow. Theſe rents are from two to ſix feet wide, and of an amazing depth; reaching from the ſurface of the valley, through a body of ice many hundred fathoms thick. On throwing down a ſtone, or any other ſolid ſubſtance, we could hear the hollow murmur of its deſcent for a very long time, ſounding like far diſtant waves breaking upon rocks.

Our guides, emboldened by habit, ſkipped over theſe rents without any ſign of fear, though they informed us, that they had often ſeen freſh clefts formed, while they walked on the valley. They added, indeed, for our encouragement, that this was always preceded by a loud continued noiſe, which gave warning of what was to happen.

It

It is evident, however, that this warning, though it should always precede the rent, could be of little use to those who had advanced to the middle of the valley; for they neither could know certainly in what direction to run, nor could they have time to get off: and in case the ice should yawn directly under their feet, they must inevitably perish.—But probably few accidents of that kind happen; and this has greater influence, than any reasoning upon the subject.

It is supposed, that the snow and ice at the bottom melting by the warmth of the earth, leave great vacancies, in the form of vaults. These natural arches support for a long time an amazing weight of ice and snow;—for there is a vast distance from the bottom to the surface of this valley.——But the ice beneath continuing to dissolve, and the snow above to increase,

the

the arches muſt at laſt give way, which occaſions the noiſe and rents above mentioned. Water, alſo, which may have fallen from the ſurface into the clefts, or is lodged by any means in this great maſs of ſnow, will, by its ſudden expanſion in the act of freezing, occaſion new rents at the ſurface.

We had heard a great deal of the havoc made by avalanches. Theſe are formed of ſnow driven by the winds againſt the higheſt and moſt protuberant parts of rocks and mountains, where it hardens and adheres ſometimes till a prodigious maſs is accumulated. But when theſe ſupporters are able to ſuſtain the increaſing weight no longer, the avalanche falls at once, hurrying large portions of the looſened rock or mountain along with it;——and rolling from a vaſt height, with a thundering noiſe, to the valley, involves in certain deſtruction

struction all the trees, houses, cattle, and men, which lie in its way *.

The greater part of those who have made a journey to the Glaciers have seen one or more of these avalanches in the very act of falling, and have themselves always escaped by miracle.——Just as most people who have made a single voyage by sea, if it were only between Dover and Calais, have met with a storm, and very narrowly escaped shipwreck.

All that any of our party can boast is, that during the nights we lay at Chamouni, we frequently heard a noise like distant thunder, which we were told was occasioned by the falling of some of these same

---

* Ac veluti montis Saxum de vertice præceps
Cum ruit avulsum vento, seu turbidus imber
Proluit, aut annis solvit sublapsa vetustas:
Fertur in abruptum magno mons improbus actu,
Exultatque solo, silvas, armenta, virosque
Involvens secum.   V<small>IRG</small>.

avalanches

avalanches at a few miles diftance. And during our excurfions, we faw trees deftroyed, and tracts of foil torn from the fides of the mountains, over which the avalanches were faid to have rolled, two or three years before we paffed. Thefe were the narroweft efcapes we made.——— I heartily wifh the fame good luck to all travellers, whatever account they themfelves may choofe to give to their friends, when they return.

The Valley of Ice is feveral leagues in length, and not above a quarter of a league in breadth. It divides into branches, which run behind the chain of mountains formerly taken notice of. It appears like a frozen amphitheatre, and is bounded by mountains, in whofe clefts columns of cryftal, as we were informed, are to be found.—The hoary majefty of Mount Blanc * * * * * * * I was in danger of rifing into poetry, when recollecting the ftory of Icarus, I thought

thought it beſt not to truſt to my own waxen wings.—I beg leave rather to borrow the following lines, which will pleaſe you better than any flight of mine, and prevent me from a fall:

So Zembla's rocks (the beauteous work of froſt)
Riſe white in air, and glitter o'er the coaſt,
Pale ſuns, unfelt, at diſtance roll away,
And on th' impaſſive lightnings play;
Eternal ſnows the growing maſs ſupply,
Fill the bright mountains, prop th' incumbent ſky;
As Atlas fix'd, each hoary pile appears,
The gather'd winter of a thouſand years.

Having walked a confiderable time on the valley, and being ſufficiently regaled with ice, we at length thought of returning to our cottage at Prieuré. Our guides led us down by a ſhorter and ſteeper way than that by which we had aſcended; and in about two hours after we had begun our deſcent, we found ourſelves at the bottom of the mountain. This rapid manner of defcending, moſt people find more fevere upon the mufcles of the legs and thighs, than even the afcent. For my own part, I was very near exhaufted; and as we were ſtill a couple of miles diftant from our lodgings, it was with the greateſt fatisfaction that I faw our obfequious mules in waiting to carry us to our cottage; where having at laſt arrived, and being affembled in a fmall room, excluded from the view of icy valleys, cryſtal hills, and fnowy mountains, with nothing before us but humble objects, as cold meat, coarfe bread, and poor wine, we contrived to pafs an hour before going to bed, in talking over the exploits of the day, and the wonders we had feen.—Whether there is greater pleafure in this, or in viewing the fcenes themfelves, is a queſtion not yet decided by the cafuiſts.

LETTER XXVI.

Geneva.

THERE are five or six different Glaciers, which all terminate upon one side of the valley of Chamouni, within the space of about five leagues.

These are prodigious collections of snow and ice, formed in the intervals or hollows, between the mountains that bound the side of the valley near which Mont Blanc stands.

The snow in those hollows being screened from the influence of the sun, the heat of summer can dissolve only a certain portion of it. These magazines of ice and snow are not formed by what falls directly from the heavens into the intervals. They are supplied

supplied by the snow which falls during winter on the loftiest parts of Mont Blanc; large beds or strata of which slide down imperceptibly by their own gravity, and finding no resistance at these intervals, they form long irregular roots around all the adjacent mountains.

Five of these enter, by five different embouchures, into the valley of Chamouni, and are called Glaciers, on one of which we had been.

At present their surface is from a thousand, to two thousand feet high, above the valley.

Their breadth depends on the wideness of the interval between the mountains in which they are formed.

Viewed from the valley, they have, in my opinion, a much finer effect than from their summit.

The rays of the fun ſtriking with various force on the different parts, according as they are more or lefs expoſed, occaſion an unequal diſſolution of the ice; and, with the help of a little imagination, give the appearances of columns, arches, and turrets, which are in ſome places tranſparent.

A fabric of ice in this taſte, two thouſand feet high, and three times as broad, with the ſun ſhining full upon it, you muſt acknowledge to be a very ſingular piece of architecture.

Our company aſcended only the Glacier of Montanvert, which is not the higheſt, and were contented with a view of the others from the valley: but more curious travellers will ſurely think it worth their labour, to examine each of them more particularly.

Some

Some people are so fond of Glaciers, that not satisfied with their present size, they insist positively, that they must necessarily grow larger every year, and they argue the matter thus:

The present existence of the Glaciers is a sufficient proof that there has, at some period or other, been a greater quantity of snow formed during the winter, than the heat of the summer has been able to dissolve. But this disproportion must necessarily increase every year, and, of consequence, the Glaciers must augment: because, any given quantity of snow and ice remaining through the course of one summer, must increase the cold of the atmosphere around it in some degree; which being reinforced by the snows of the succeeding winter, will resist the dissolving power of the sun more the second summer than the first, and still more the third than the second, and so on.

The conclufion of this reafoning is, that the Glaciers muft grow larger by an increafing ratio every year, till the end of time. For this reafon, the authors of this theory regret, that they themfelves have been fent into the world fo foon; becaufe, if their birth had been delayed for nine or ten thoufand years, they fhould have feen the Glaciers in much greater glory, Mont Blanc being but a Lilliputian at prefent, in comparifon of what it will be then.

However rational this may appear, objections have neverthelefs been fuggefted, which I am forry for; becaufe, when a theory is tolerably confiftent, well fabricated, and goodly to behold, nothing can be more vexatious, than to fee a plodding officious fellow overthrow the whole ftructure at once, by a dafh of his pen, as harlequin does a houfe with a touch of his fword, in a pantomime entertainment.

Such

MANNERS IN FRANCE, &c. 233

Such cavillers fay, that as the Glaciers augment in fize, there muft be a greater extent of furface for the fun-beams to act upon, and, of confequence, the diffolution will be greater, which muft effectually prevent the continual increafe contended for.

But the other party extricate themfelves from this difficulty by roundly afferting, that the additional cold occafioned by the fnow and ice already depofited, has a much greater influence in retarding their diffolution, than the increafed furface can have in haftening it: and in confirmation of their fyftem, they tell you, that the oldeft inhabitants of Chamouni remember the Glaciers when they were much fmaller than at prefent; and alfo remember the time when they could walk, from the Valley of Ice, to places behind the mountains, by paffages which are now quite choked up with hills of fnow, not above fifty years old.

Whether

Whether the inhabitants of Chamouni assert this from a laudable partiality to the Glaciers, whom they may now consider, (on account of their drawing strangers to visit the Valley) as their best neighbours;— or from politeness to the supporters of the above-mentioned opinion;—or from real observation, I shall not presume to say.— But I myself have heard several of the old people in Chamouni assert the fact.

The cavillers being thus obliged to relinquish their former objection, attempt, in the next place, to show, that the above theory leads to an absurdity; because, say they, If the Glaciers go on increasing in bulk ad infinitum, the globe itself would become in process of time a mere appendage to Mont Blanc.

The advocates for the continual augmentation of the Glaciers reply, that as this inconveniency has not already happened,

pened, there needs no other refutation of the impious doctrine of certain philosophers, who affert that the world has existed from eternity; and as to the globe's becoming an appendage to the mountain, they affure us, that the world will be at an end long before that event can happen. So that those of the moft timid natures, and moft delicate conftitutions, may difmifs their fears on that fubject.

For my own part, though I wifh well to the Glaciers, and all the inhabitants of Chamouni, having paffed fome days very pleafantly in their company; I will take no part in this controverfy, the merits of which I leave to your own judgment.

LETTER XXVII.

Geneva.

THE morning of the day on which we departed from Prieuré, I obferved a girl of a very fingular appearance fitting before the door of one of the houfes. When I fpoke to her, fhe made no anfwer: But an elderly man, who had been a foldier in the king of Sardinia's fervice, and my acquaintance fince the moment of our arrival, informed me, that this girl was an ideot, and had been fo from her birth.

He took me to two other houfes in the village, in each of which there was one perfon in the fame melancholy fituation ; and he affured me, that all over the valley of Chamouni, in a family confifting of five or

fix

six children, one of them, generally speaking, was a perfect natural.

This was confirmed by some others, to whom I afterwards mentioned it. I was told at the same time, that the parents, so far from considering this as a misfortune, looked upon it as an indication of good luck to the rest of the family, and no unhappiness to the individual, whom they always cherish and protect with the utmost tenderness.

I asked my soldier, if any of his own family were in that situation? Non, Monsieur, answered he; et aussi j'ai passé une vie bien dure.

Don't you think these poor creatures very unhappy?

Demande pardon, Monsieur:—Ils sont très heureux——

But

But you would not like to have been born in that ſtate yourſelf?

Vous croyez donc, Monſieur, que j'aurois été bien attrapé?

Attrapé!—certainly:—don't you think ſo too?

Pour cela, non, Monſieur; je n'aurois jamais travaillé.——

To one who has through life been obliged to work hard for a bare ſubſiſtence, labour appears the greateſt evil, and perfect idleneſs the greateſt bleſſing. If this ſoldier had been brought up in idleneſs, and had experienced all the horrors and dejection which attend indolent luxury, very poſſibly he would be of a different opinion.

During this journey, I remarked, that in ſome particular villages, and for a conſiderable tract of country, ſcarcely was there any

any body to be seen who had that swelling of the throat and neck, which is thought so general among all the inhabitants of the Alps. In particular, I did not observe any body at Prieuré with this complaint; and, upon enquiry, was informed, that there are many parishes in which not a single person is troubled with it, and that in other places at no great distance it is almost universal.

In the valley of Chamouni there is only one hamlet where it is common; but in the Pays de Vallais, I was told, it is more frequent than in any other place.

As this disease seems to be endemical, it cannot, as has been imagined, proceed from the drinking of water impregnated with snow or ice; for this beverage is common to all the inhabitants of the Alps, and of other mountains.

If

If the water be in reality the vehicle of this difeafe, we muft fuppofe it impregnated not only with diffolved ice and fnow, but alfo with fome falt, or other fubftance, poffeffed of the noxious quality of obftructing the glands of the throat; and we muft alfo fuppofe, that this noxious fubftance is to be found in no other inhabited place but the Alps.

After one of the inhabitants of Chamouni had enumerated many parifhes where there were, and others where there were no Guatres (which is the name they give this fwelling), he concluded by telling me, I fhould fee them in great abundance among the Valaifans, to whofe country we were going.—When I told the man, I thought his country-people very happy, in being quite free from fuch an odious difeafe, which afflicted their poor neighbours——En revenche, faid the peafant, nous fommes accablés

accablés des impôts;—et dans le pays de Vallais on ne paye rien.

The d——l is in the fellow, exclaimed I.—Were it in your choice, would you accept of Guatres, to get free of taxes?

Très volontiers, Monſieur;—l'un vaut bien l'autre.

> Quid cauſæ eſt, merito quin illis Jupiter ambas,
> Iratas buccas inflet.

You ſee, my friend, that it is not in courts and capitals alone that men are diſcontented with their fortunes. The cauſes of repining are different in different places; but the effect is the ſame every where.

On the morning of the ſixth day, we bid adieu to Prieuré; and having aſcended the mountains, which ſhut up the valley of Chamouni at the end oppoſite to that by which

which we had entered, after various windings on a very rugged road, we gradually defcended into a hollow of the moft difmal appearance.

It is furrounded with high, bare, rugged rocks, without trees or verdure of any kind, the bottom being as barren and craggy as the fides, and the whole forming a moft hideous landfcape. This dreary valley is of a confiderable length, but very narrow. I imagine it would have pleafed the fancy of Salvator, who might have been tempted to fteal a corner of it for one of his pieces, which, when he had enlivened with a murder or two, would have been a mafter-piece of the Horrible.

Having traverfed this, we continued our journey, fometimes afcending, then defcending into other vallies whofe names I have forgot.—We had a long continued afcent over Mont Noir, a very high hill, covered

covered with pine-trees, many of which are above a hundred feet in height. I was obliged to walk on foot moſt of this road, which is full as ſteep as any part of that by which we had aſcended Montanvert.

We came at length to the paſs which ſeparates the King of Sardinia's country from the little republic, called the Pays de Vallais. Acroſs this there is an old thick wall, and a gate, without any guard. This narrow paſs continues for ſeveral miles.— A few peaſants arranged along the upper part of the mountains could, by rolling down ſtones, deſtroy a whole army, if it ſhould attempt to enter into the country by this road.

When you have paſſed through this long defile, the road runs along the ſide of a high and ſteep mountain; but is ſtill ſo very narrow, that two perſons cannot with ſafety go abreaſt, and all paſſengers are en- tirely

tirely at the mercy of thofe who may be pofted on the higher parts of the mountain.

From the fide of the mountain on which we paffed, we could have fpoken to the people who inhabited the fide of the mountain oppofite. But I am convinced it would have taken three or four hours walking, to have gone to them: Becaufe we muft, by a long, oblique tour, have firft reached the bottom of the cleft between us, and then have afcended to them by another long, fatiguing path, which could not be done in lefs time than I have mentioned.

Wherever there is a fpot of the mountain tolerably fertile, and the flope lefs formidable than ufual, you are almoft certain to find a peafant's houfe. All the houfes are built of the fine red pine, which grows near at hand. The carriage of this, even for a fhort way, upon thofe very fteep mountains, muft have been attended with

no

no small difficulty and danger. These dwellings are raised on wooden props, or pillars, two or three feet above the ground. On the top of each pillar a large flag or broad stone is placed, to obstruct the entrance of rats.—Indeed the situation of these abodes is so very aerial, that they seem almost inaccessible to every animal that has not wings, as well as to rats.

The road led us at length to the summit, which is level, and covered with pines for several miles. Having traversed this, and descended a little on the other side, the lower Vallais opened to our view. Nothing can be imagined more singularly picturesque;—It is of an oval form, about seven leagues in length, and one in breadth, surrounded on all sides by mountains of a stupendous height, the lower parts of which are covered with very rich pasture.—The valley itself is fertile in the highest degree, finely cultivated, and divided into meadows, gardens,

gardens, and vineyards. The Rhone flows in beautiful mazes from the one end to the other.—Sion, the capital of the Vallais, is situated on the upper extremity, and the town of Martigny on the lower, many villages and detached houses appearing all over the valley between them. The prospect we had now under our eye formed a striking and agreeable contrast with the scenes we had just left. The distance from this point to Martigny, which stands near the bottom of the mountain, is about six miles. There is one continued descent the whole way, which is rendered easy by the roads being thrown into a zig-zag direction.

After the rugged paths we had been accustomed to, it was, comparatively speaking, rest, to walk down this mountain.— We arrived at Martigny refreshed, and in high spirits.

LETTTER XXVIII.

Geneva.

DURING our journey over the mountains which encircle the lower Vallais, I had often felt an inclination to enter some of the peasants' houses, that I might be a witness of the domestic œconomy of a people which Rousseau has so delightfully described.

Had I been alone, or with a single companion, I should have pledged them liberally, and made a temporary sacrifice of my reason to the Penates of those happy mountaineers; for, according to him, this is the only payment they will receive for their entertainment: But our company was by far

far too numerous, and would have put their hospitality to too severe a trial.

After a night's refreshment at Martigny, we looked with some degree of impatience for the cabriolets, which had been ordered to meet us there. We all talked with rapture of the sublime scenes from which we had descended; yet nobody regretted that the rest of the journey was to be performed on plain ground. The cabriolets arriving the same forenoon, we set out by the *embouchure*, which leads to St. Maurice.

That immense rampart of mountains which surrounds the Vallais at every other part, is cut through here, which renders that country accessible to the inhabitants of the canton of Bern. This opening has the appearance of a vast and magnificent avenue, on each side of which a row of lofty mountains are placed, inſtead of trees. It is ſome leagues in length. The ground is exceedingly fertile, and perfectly level: Yet if an attack were ſuſpected, this paſs could be eaſily defended by batteries at the bottom of the mountains on each ſide. Beſides, a river of conſiderable depth flows along, ſometimes on the one ſide, and ſometimes on the other, and, by continually croſſing the plain, ſeems to forbid all hoſtile incroachments.

This little ſpot, the country of the Vallaiſans, which comprehends the valley above deſcribed, the mountains that ſurround it, and ſtretch on one ſide all the way to the lake, including three or four towns and many villages, is a diſtrict, governed by its own laws and magiſtrates, in alliance with, but independent of, the Swiſs cantons, or any other power. The religion is popery, and the form of government democratic.— It ſeems to have been imagined by Nature as a laſt aſylum for that divinity, without whoſe

whose influence all her other gifts are of
small value. Should the rapacious hand of
despotism ever crush the rights of mankind, and overturn the altars of FREEDOM,
in every other country in Europe, a chosen
people may here preserve the true worship,
and share her regard with the provinces
beyond the Atlantic.

In the middle of the opening above mentioned, about four leagues from Martigny,
between two high mountains, and at the
side of the Rhone, is situated the little town
of St. Maurice, which guards this entrance
into the lower Vallais.

Having passed a bridge at this town,
which divides the country of the Vallaisans
from the canton of Bern, we proceeded to
Bex, a village remarkable for its delightful situation, and for the salt-works which
are near it. After dinner, we visited these.
We entered the largest saline by a passage
cut

cut out of the folid rock, of a fufficient height and breadth to allow a man to walk with eafe.

Travellers who have the curiofity to explore thefe gloomy abodes, are previoufly furnifhed with lighted lamps or torches, and dreffed in a coarfe habit, to defend them from the flimy drippings which fall from the roof and fides of the paffage.

Upon arriving at the refervoir of falt water, which is about three quarters of a mile from the entrance, I was feized with a naufea, from the difagreeable fmell of the place, and returned with all poffible expedition to the open air, leaving my companions to pufh their refearches as far as they pleafed. They remained a confiderable time after me. What fatisfaction they received within, I fhall not take upon me to determine; but I never faw a fet of people make a more melancholy exit;—with

their

their greafy frocks, their torches, their fmoky, woe-begone countenances, they put me in mind of a proceffion of condemned heretics, walking to the flames, at an Auto de Fè at Lifbon.

Having recovered their looks and fpirits at the inn at Bex, they affured me, that the curiofities they had feen during their fubterraneous progrefs, particularly after my feceffion, were more worthy of obfervation than any thing we had met with fince we had left Geneva; and they all advifed me, with affected ferioufnefs, to return and complete the interefting vifit which I had left unfinifhed.

Next morning our company divided, the D— of H—— and Mr. G—— chufing to return by Vevay and Laufanne. Mr. U—, Mr. K—, and myfelf, went by the other fide of the lake of Geneva. They took with them the two chaifes, and we proceeded

ceeded on horſeback, our road not admitting of wheel-carriages.

We left Bex early in the morning, paſſing through Aigle, a thriving little town, whoſe houſes are built of a white marble found in the neighbourhood.—The ideas of gloom and wretchedneſs, as well as of magnificence, had ſomehow been linked in my mind with this ſubſtance.—I don't know whether this has been owing to its being uſed in tombs and monuments;—or to my having obſerved, that the houſes moſt profuſely ornamented by it are ſo often the manſions of dulneſs and diſcontent.— Whatever gave riſe to this connection of ideas, the appearance of the inhabitants of Aigle was well calculated to cure me of the prejudice; for although the meaneſt houſes in this poor little town are built of marble, yet in the courſe of my life I never beheld leſs care and more ſatisfaction in the countenances of any ſet of people.

people. An appearance of eafe and content not only prevails here, but all over Switzerland.

A little beyond Aigle, we croffed the Rhone in boats. It is broader at this ferry, than where it flows from the lake of Geneva. As foon as we arrived on the other fide, we were again in the dominions of the Vallaifans, which extend on this fide all the way to the lake.

We had a delightful ride to St. Gingo, where we dined, and remained feveral hours to refrefh our horfes. Though it was Sunday, there was a fair at this town, to which fuch a concourfe of people had reforted from the Pays de Valais, the canton of Bern, and from Savoy, that we could not without difficulty find a room to dine in.

The

The dreſs of the young Vallaiſannes is remarkably picturesque. A little ſilk hat, fixed on one ſide of the head, from which a bunch of ribbons hangs negligently, with a jacket very advantageous to the ſhape, gives them a ſmart air, and is upon the whole more becoming than the dreſs of the common people in any country I have yet ſeen.

A little beyond St. Gingo, we entered the dukedom of Savoy. The road is here cut out of the lofty rocks which riſe from the lake of Geneva. It muſt be paſſed with caution, being exceedingly narrow, and no fence to prevent the traveller from falling over a very high precipice into the lake, in caſe his horſe ſhould ſtart to one ſide.

At ſome places this narrow road is rendered ſtill more dangerous by fragments which have fallen from the mountains above, and have impaired and almoſt deſtroyed ftroyed the path. At thofe places we were obliged to difmount, and lead our horfes, with great attention, over rubbifh and broken rocks, till we gained thofe parts of the road which were intire.

The fight of Meillerie brought to my remembrance the charming letters of Rouffeau's two lovers. This recollection filled me with a pleafing enthufiafm. I fought with my eyes, and imagined I difcovered the identical place where St. Preux fat with his telefcope to view the habitation of his beloved Julia.—I traced in my imagination his route, when he fprung from rock to rock after one of her letters, which a fudden guft of wind had fnatched from his hands.—I marked the point at which the two lovers embarked to return to Clarence, after an evening vifit to thofe very rocks,— when St. Preux, agonized with tender recollections, and diftracted with defpair, was tempted to feize his miftrefs, then the wife of of another, and precipitate himself along with her, from the boat headlong into the middle of the lake.

Every circumstance of that pathetic story came fresh into my mind. I felt myself on a kind of classic ground, and experienced that the eloquence of that inimitable writer had given me an interest in the landscape before my eyes, beyond that which its own natural beauties could have effected.

Having left the romantic rocks of Meillerie behind, we descended to a fertile plain, almost on a level with the lake; along which the road runs, flanked with rows of fine tall trees all the way to Evian, an agreeable little town, renowned for its mineral waters. Here we met with many of our Geneva acquaintances of both sexes, who had come, under pretence of drinking the waters, to amuse themselves in this delightful retreat.

We next proceeded to Tonon, a moſt religious city, if we may judge by the number of churches and monaſteries which it contains. The number of inhabitants are calculated at ſix or ſeven thouſand, and every ſeventh perſon I ſaw wore the uniform of ſome religious order. After this, I was not greatly ſurpriſed to perceive every ſymptom of poverty among the lay inhabitants.

Having beſpoke ſupper and beds at this place, we went and viſited the convent of Carthuſians at Repaille, which is at a little diſtance.

It was here that a Duke of Savoy, after a fortunate reign, aſſumed the character of a hermit, and lived with the fathers a life of piety and mortification, according to ſome; of voluptuouſneſs and policy, according to others. What we are well aſſured of is, that he was in a ſhort time elected

elected Pope, by the council of Bafil, which dignity he was obliged to relinquifh nine years after, having firft made very honourable conditions for himfelf. After this, he fpent the remainder of his life with the reputation of great fanctity at Repaille.

Had he been allowed to chufe any part of Europe for his retreat, he could not have found one more agreeable than this which his own dominions furnifhed.

The fathers with great politenefs fhowed us their foreft, their gardens, their apartments, and a very elegant new chapel, which is juft finifhed. They then conducted us into the chamber where their Sovereign had ived and died. They talked much of his ;enius, his benevolence, and his fanctity. We heard them with every mark of acquifcence, and returned to our inn, where ho' *we* certainly did not *faire Repaille*, I'm convinced the fleas did: As Shakefpeare's

carrier

carrier fays, there was never a King in Chriftendom better bit than we were, through the whole night. We paid for our entertainment, fuch as it was, a very extravagant bill in the morning, and without grudging; for we confidered, that we were to leave our hoft and his family amongft a fwarm of blood-fuckers, ftill more intolerable than fleas.

We arrived the fame forenoon at Geneva, having finifhed a tour in which a greater variety of fublime and interefting objects offer themfelves to the contemplation of the traveller, than can be found in any other part of the globe of the fame extent.

I am, &c.

LETTER XXIX.

Geneva.

I Am not furprifed that your inquiries of late entirely regard the philofopher of Ferney. This extraordinary perfon has contrived to excite more curiofity, and to retain the attention of Europe for a longer fpace of time, than any other man this age has produced, monarchs and heroes included.——Even the moft trivial anecdote relating to him feems, in fome degree, to intereft the Public.

Since I have been in this country, I have had frequent opportunities of converfing with him, and ftill more with thofe who have lived in intimacy with him for many years; fo that, whatever remarks I may fend you on this subject, are founded either on my own obfervation, or on that of the moſt candid and intelligent of his acquaintance.

He has enemies and admirers here, as he has every where elſe; and not unfrequently both united in the ſame perſon.

The firſt idea which has preſented itſelf to all who have attempted a deſcription of his perſon, is that of a ſkeleton. In as far as this implies exceſſive leanneſs, it is juſt; but it muſt be remembered, that this ſkeleton, this mere compoſition of ſkin and bone, has a look of more ſpirit and vivacity, than is generally produced by fleſh and blood, however blooming and youthful.

The moſt piercing eyes I ever beheld are thoſe of Voltaire, now in his eightieth year. His whole countenance is expreſ-
five

five of genius, obfervation, and extreme fenfibility.

In the morning he has a look of anxiety and difcontent; but this gradually wears off, and after dinner he feems cheerful:— yet an air of irony never entirely forfakes his face, but may always be obferved lurking in his features, whether he frowns or fmiles.

When the weather is favourable, he takes an airing in his coach, with his niece, or with fome of his guefts, of whom there is always a fufficient number at Ferney. Sometimes he faunters in his garden; or if the weather does not permit him to go abroad, he employs his leifure-hours in playing at chefs with Pere Adam; or in receiving the vifits of ftrangers, a continual fucceffion of whom attend at Ferney to catch an opportunity of feeing him; or in dictating and reading letters; for he ftill retains

retains correspondents in all the countries of Europe, who inform him of every remarkable occurrence, and send him every new literary production as soon as it appears.

By far the greater part of his time is spent in his study; and whether he reads himself, or listens to another, he always has a pen in his hand, to take notes, or make remarks.

Composition is his principal amusement. No author who writes for daily bread, no young poet ardent for distinction, is more assiduous with his pen, or more anxious for fresh fame, than the wealthy and applauded Seigneur of Ferney.

He lives in a very hospitable manner, and takes care always to keep a good cook. He has generally two or three visitors from Paris, who stay with him a month or six weeks.

at

at a time. When they go, their places are soon supplied; so that there is a constant rotation of society at Ferney. These, with Voltaire's own family, and his visitors from Geneva, compose a company of twelve or fourteen people, who dine daily at his table, whether he appears or not. For when engaged preparing some new production for the press, indisposed or in bad spirits, he does not dine with the company; but satisfies himself with seeing them for a few minutes, either before or after dinner.

All who bring recommendations from his friends, may depend upon being received, if he be not really indisposed.—He often presents himself to the strangers, who assemble almost every afternoon in his antichamber, although they bring no particular recommendation. But sometimes they are obliged to retire without having their curiosity gratified.

As often as this happens, he is fure of being accufed of peevifhnefs; and a thoufand ill-natured ftories are related, perhaps invented, out of revenge, becaufe he is not in the humour of being exhibited like a dancing-bear on a holiday. It is much lefs furprifing that he fometimes refufes, than that he fhould comply fo often. In him, this complaifance muft proceed folely from a defire to oblige; for Voltaire has been fo long accuftomed to admiration, that the ftare of a few ftrangers cannot be fuppofed to afford him much pleafure.

His niece, Madame Denis, does the honours of the table, and entertains the company, when her uncle is not able, or does not choofe to appear. She is a well-difpofed woman, who behaves with good-humour to every body, and with unremitting attention and tendernefs to her uncle.

The forenoon is not a proper time to vifit Voltaire. He cannot bear to have his hours

hours of ſtudy interrupted. This alone is ſufficient to put him in bad humour; beſides, he is then apt to be querulous, whether he ſuffers by the infirmities of age or from ſome accidental cauſe of chagrin. Whatever is the reaſon, he is leſs an optimiſt at that part of the day than at any other.——It was in the morning, probably, that he remarked,——que c'etoit domage que le quinquina ſe trouvoit en Amérique, et la fiévre en nos climats.

Thoſe who are invited to ſupper, have an opportunity of ſeeing him in the moſt advantageous point of view. He then exerts himſelf to entertain the company, and ſeems as fond of ſaying, what are called good things, as ever:——and when any lively remark or bon mot comes from another, he is equally delighted, and pays the fulleſt tribute of applauſe.——The ſpirit of mirth gains upon him by indulgence.—When ſurrounded by his friends, and animated by the preſence of women, he he seems to enjoy life with all the sensibility of youth. His genius then surmounts the restraints of age and infirmity, and flows along in a fine strain of pleasing, spirited observation, and delicate irony.

He has an excellent talent of adapting his conversation to his company.—The first time the D— of H—— waited on him, he turned the discourse on the ancient alliance between the French and Scotch nations.— Reciting the circumstance of one of his Grace's predecessors having accompanied Mary Queen of Scots, whose heir he at that time was, to the court of France,— he spoke of the heroic characters of his ancestors, the ancient Earls of Douglas— of the great literary reputation of some of his countrymen, then living; and mentioned the names of Hume and Robertson in terms of high approbation.

A short time afterwards, he was visited by two Russian Noblemen, who are now

at

at Geneva. Voltaire talked to them a great deal of their Emprefs, and the flourifhing ftate of their country.——Formerly, faid he, your countrymen were guided by ignorant priefts,—the arts were unknown, and your lands lay wafte;—but now the arts flourifh, and the lands are cultivated.— One of the young men replied, That there was ftill a great proportion of barren land in Ruffia.—At leaft, faid Voltaire, you muft admit, that of late your country has been very *fertile in laurels.*

His diflike to the clergy is well known.— This leads him to join in a very trite topic of abufe with people who have no pretenfion to that degree of wit which alone could make their railings tolerable.—The converfation happening to turn into this channel, one perfon faid, If you fubftract pride from priefts, nothing will remain.— Vous comptez donc, Monfieur, la gourmandife, pour rien, faid Voltaire.

He

He approves much more of Marmontel's Art of Poetry, than of any poems of that author's compofition. Speaking of thefe, he faid that Marmontel, like Mofes, could guide others to the Holy Land, though he was not allowed to enter it himfelf*.

Voltaire's unbecoming allufions to the Sacred Writings, and his attempts to turn into ridicule fome of the moft venerable characters mentioned in them, are notorious.

A certain perfon, who ftammered very much, found means to get himfelf introduced at Ferney.——He had no other recommendation than the praifes he very liberally beftowed on himfelf.——When

* The fame allufion, though probably Voltaire did not know it, was long fince made by Cowley—
Bacon like Mofes led us forth at laft
The barren wildernefs he paft,
Did on the very border ftand
Of the bleft promifed land,
And from the mountain top of his exalted wit
Saw it himfelf, and fhewed us it.

he

he left the room, Voltaire faid, he fuppofed him to be an avanturier, un impofteur.—Madame Denis faid, Impoftors never ftammer:—To which Voltaire replied—Moïfe, ne begayoit-il pas ?

You muft have heard of the animofity which has long fubfifted between Voltaire and Freron the Journalift at Paris. The former was walking one day in his garden with a gentleman from Geneva. A toad crawled acrofs the road before them:—The gentleman, to pleafe Voltaire, faid, pointing at the toad,—There is a Freron.—What can that poor animal have done to you, replied the Wit, to deferve fuch a name ?

He compared the Britifh nation to a hogfhead of their own ftrong beer; the top of which is froth, the bottom dregs, the middle excellent.

A friend of Voltaire's having recommended to his perufal, a particular fyftem of of metaphyfics, fupported by a train of reafonings, by which the author difplayed his own ingenuity and addrefs, without convincing the mind of the reader, or proving any thing befides his own eloquence and fophiftry, afked, fome time after, the critic's opinion of this performance?

Metaphyfical writers, replied Voltaire, are like minuet-dancers; who being dreffed to the greateft advantage, make a couple of bows, move through the room in the fineft attitudes, difplay all their graces, are in continual motion without advancing a ftep, and finifh at the identical point from which they fet out. ✕

This, I hope, will fatisfy you for the prefent; in my next, I fhall fend you what farther particulars I think worth your notice concerning this fingular man.—Mean while, I am, &c.

✝ Or placed in Metaphysic ground to prance,
show all his paces, ne'er one step advance.

LETTER XXX.

Geneva.

COnsidered as a master, Voltaire appears in a very amiable light. He is affable, humane, and generous to his tenants and dependants. He loves to see them prosper; and takes part in their private and domestic concerns, with the attention of a patriarch.—He promotes industry and manufactures among them, by every means he can devise: by his care and patronage alone, Ferney, from a wretched village, whose inhabitants were sunk in sloth and poverty, is become a flourishing and commodious little town.

That acrimony, which appears in some of Voltaire's works, seems to be excited only against rival wits, and cotemporary writers,

writers, who refufe him that diftinguifhed place on Parnaffus, to which his talents entitle him.

If he has been the author of fevere fatire, he has alfo been the object of a great deal. Who has been the aggreffor, it would be difficult to determine; but it muft be confeffed, that where he has not been irritated as a writer, he appears a good-humoured man; and, in particular inftances, difplays a true philanthropy.——The whole of his conduct refpecting the Calas family;—his protection of the Sirvens, his patronage of the young lady defcended from Corneille, and many examples, which might be mentioned, are all of this nature.

Some people will tell you, that all the buftle he made, on thefe, and fimilar occafions, proceeded from vanity; but in my mind, the man who takes pains to juftify oppreffed innocence, to roufe the indignation

tion of mankind againſt cruelty, and to relieve indigent merit, is in reality benevolent, however vain he may be of ſuch actions.——Such a man is unqueſtionably a more uſeful member of ſociety, than the humbleſt monk, who has no other plan in life, than the working out his own ſalvation in a corner.

Voltaire's criticiſms on the writings of Shakeſpear do him no honour; they betray an ignorance of the author, whoſe works he ſo raſhly condemns. Shakeſpear's irregularities, and his difregard for the unities of the drama, are obvious to the dulleſt of modern critics; but Voltaire's national prejudices, and his imperfect knowledge of the language, render him blind to ſome of the moſt ſhining beauties of the Engliſh Poet; his remarks, however, though not always candid nor delicate, are for the moſt part lively.

One evening, at Ferney, the conversation happening to turn on the genius of Shakefpear, Voltaire expatiated on the impropriety and abfurdity of introducing low characters and vulgar dialogue into Tragedy; and gave many inftances of the Englifh bard's having offended in that particular, even in his moft pathetic plays. A gentleman of the company, who is a great admirer of Shakefpear, obferved, by way of palliation, that though thofe characters were low, yet they were natural (dans la nature, was his expreffion). Avec permiffion, Monfieur, replied Voltaire, mon cul eft bien dans la nature, et cependant je porte de coulottes.

Voltaire had formerly a little theatre at his own houfe, where dramatic pieces were reprefented by fome of the fociety who vifited there, he himfelf generally taking fome important character; but by all accounts this was not his fort, nature having
fitted

fitted him for conceiving the fentiments, but not reprefenting the actions of a hero.

Mr. Cramer of Geneva fometimes affifted upon thefe occafions.——I have often feen that gentleman act at a private theatre in that city with deferved applaufe. Very few of thofe who have made acting the ftudy and bufinefs of their lives, could have reprefented the characters in which he appeared, with more judgment and energy.

The celebrated Clairon herfelf has been proud to tread Voltaire's domeftic theatre, and to difplay at once his genius and her own.

Thefe dramatic entertainments at Ferney, to which many of the inhabitants of Geneva were, from time to time, invited, in all probability increafed their defire for fuch amufements, and gave the hint to a

company

company of French comedians, to come every fummer to the neighbourhood.

As the Syndics and Council did not judge it proper to licenfe their acting, this company have erected a theatre at Chatelaine, which is on the French fide of the ideal line which feparates that kingdom from the territories of the Republic, and about three miles from the ramparts of Geneva.

People come occafionally from Savoy and Switzerland to attend thefe reprefentations; but the company on which the actors chiefly depend, are the citizens of Geneva. The play begins at three or four in the afternoon, that the fpectators may have time to return before the fhutting of the gates.

I have been frequently at this theatre. The performers are moderately good. The admired Le Kain, who is now at Ferney, on a vifit to Voltaire, fometimes exhibits:

hibits:—but when I go, my chief inducement is to fee Voltaire, who generally attends when Le Kain acts, and when one of his own tragedies is to be reprefented.

He fits on the ftage, and behind the fcenes; but fo as to be feen by a great part of the audience. He takes as much intereft in the reprefentation, as if his own character depended on the performance. He feems perfectly chagrined and difgufted when any of the actors commit a miftake; and when he thinks they perform well, never fails to mark his approbation with all the violence of voice and gefture.

He enters into the feigned diftreffes of the piece with every fymptom of real emotion, and even fheds tears with the profufion of a girl prefent for the firft time at a tragedy.

I have sometimes sat near him during the whole entertainment, observing with astonishment such a degree of sensibility in a man of eighty. This great age, one would naturally believe, might have considerably blunted every sensation, particularly those occasioned by the fictitious distresses of the drama, to which he has been habituated from his youth.

The pieces represented having been wrote by himself, is another circumstance which, in my opinion, should naturally tend to prevent their effect on him. Some people indeed assert that this, so far from diminishing, is the real cause of all his sensibility; and they urge, as a proof of this assertion, that he attends the theatre only when some of his own pieces are to be acted.

That he should be better pleased to see his own tragedies represented than any others,

others, is natural; but I do not readily comprehend, how he can be more easily moved and deceived, by distresses which he himself invented. Yet this degree of deception seems necessary to make a man shed tears. While these tears are flowing, he must believe the woes he weeps are real: he must have been so far deceived by the cunning of the scene, as to have forgot that he was in a playhouse. The moment he recollects that the whole is fiction, his sympathy and tears must cease.

I should be glad, however, to see Voltaire present at the representation of some of Corneille or Racine's tragedies, that I might observe whether he would discover more or less sensibility than he has done at his own. We should then be able to ascertain this curious, disputed point, whether his sympathy regarded the piece or the author.

Happy,

Happy, if this extraordinary man had confined his genius to its native home, to the walks which the mufes love, and where he has always been received with diftinguifhed honour, and that he had never deviated from thefe, into the thorny paths of controverfy. For while he attacked the tyrants and oppreffors of mankind, and thofe who have perverted the benevolent nature of Chriftianity to the moft felfifh and malignant purpofes, it is for ever to be regretted, that he allowed the fhafts of his ridicule to glance upon the Chriftian religion itfelf.

By perfevering in this, he has not only fhocked the pious, but even difgufted infidels, who accufe him of borrowing from himfelf, and repeating the fame argument in various publications; and feem as tired of the ftale fneer againft the Chriftian doctrines, as of the dulleft and moft tedious fermons in fupport of them.

Voltaire's

Voltaire's behaviour during ficknefs has been reprefented in very oppofite lights. I have heard much of his great contrition and repentance, when he had reafon to believe his end approaching. Thefe ftories, had they been true, would have proved, that his infidelity was affectation, and that he was a believer and Chriftian in his heart.

I own I could never give any credit to fuch reports; for though I have frequently met with vain young men, who have given themfelves airs of free-thinking, while in reality they were even fuperftitious, yet I never could underftand what a man like Voltaire, or any man of common underftanding, could propofe to himfelf by fuch abfurd affectation. To pretend to defpife what we really revere, and to treat as human, what we believe to be divine, is certainly, of all kinds of hypocrify, the moft unpardonable.

I was

I was at some pains to ascertain this matter; and I have been assured, by those who have lived during many years in familiarity with him, that all these stories are without foundation. They declared, that although he was unwilling to quit the enjoyment of life, and used the means of preserving health, he seemed no way afraid of the consequences of dying. That he never discovered, either in health or sickness, any remorse for the works imputed to him against the Christian religion.——That, on the contrary, he was blinded to such a degree, as to express uneasiness at the thoughts of dying before some of them, in which he was at that time engaged, were finished.

Though this conduct is not to be justified upon any supposition, yet there is more consistency, and, in my opinion, less wickedness in it, if we admit the account which his friends give, than there would be in his writing at once against the established opinions

nions of mankind, the conviction of his own confcience, and the infpirations of the Deity, merely to acquire the applaufe of a few miftaken infidels.

However erroneous he may have been, I cannot fufpect him of fuch abfurdity. On the contrary, I imagine, that as foon as he is convinced of the truths of Chriftianity, he will openly avow his opinion, in health as in ficknefs, uniformly, to his laft moment.

LETTER XXXI.

Geneva.

IN obedience to your requeſt, I ſhall give you my opinion freely with regard to Lord ——'s ſcheme of ſending his two ſons to be educated at Geneva.

The oldeſt, if I remember right, is not more than nine years of age; and they have advanced no farther in their education than being able to read Engliſh tolerably well. His Lordſhip's idea is, that when they ſhall have acquired a perfect knowledge of the French language, they may be taught Latin through the medium of that language, and purſue any other ſtudy that may be thought proper.

I have attended to his Lordſhip's objections againſt the public ſchools in England, and after due conſideration, and weighing every circumſtance, I remain of opinion, that no country but Great Britain is proper for the education of a Britiſh ſubject, who propoſes to paſs his life in his own country. The moſt important point, in my mind, to be ſecured in the education of a young man of rank of our country, is to make him an Engliſhman; and this can be done nowhere ſo effectually as in England.

He will there acquire thoſe ſentiments, that particular taſte and turn of mind, which will make him prefer the government, and reliſh the manners, the diverſions, and general way of living, which prevail in England.

He will there acquire that character, which diſtinguiſhes Engliſhmen from the natives of all the other countries of Europe, and

and which once attained, however it may be afterwards embellished or deformed, can never be entirely effaced.

If it could be proved, that this character is not the most amiable, it does not follow that it is not the most expedient. It is sufficient, that it is upon the whole most approved of in England. For I hold it as indisputable, that the good opinion of a man's countrymen is of more importance to him than that of all the rest of mankind: Indeed, without the first, he very rarely can enjoy the other.

It is thought, that, by an early foreign education, all ridiculous English prejudices will be avoided. This may be true;—but other prejudices, perhaps as ridiculous, and much more detrimental, will be formed. The first cannot be attended with many inconveniencies; the second may render the young people unhappy in their own country

try when they return, and difagreeable to their countrymen all the reft of their lives.

It is true, that the French manners are adopted in almoft every country of Europe: they prevail all over Germany and the northern courts. They are gaining ground, though with a flower pace, in Spain, and in the Italian ftates.—This is not the cafe in England.—The Englifh manners are univerfal in the provinces, prevail in the capital, and are to be found uncontaminated even at court.

In all the countries above mentioned, the body of the people behold this preference to foreign manners with difguft. But in all thofe countries, the fentiments of the people are difregarded; whereas, in England, popularity is of real importance; and the higher a man's rank is, the more he will feel the lofs of it.

Befides, a prejudice againft French manners is not confined to the lower ranks in England:—It is diffufed over the whole nation. Even thofe who have none of the ufual prejudices;—who do all manner of juftice to the talents and ingenuity of their neighbours;—who approve of French manners in French people; yet cannot fuffer them when grafted on their countrymen. Should an Englifh gentleman think this kind of grafting at all admiffible, it will be in fome of the loweft claffes with whom he is connected, as his tailor, barber, valet-de-chambre, or cook;—but never in his friend.

I can fcarcely remember an inftance of an Englifhman of fafhion, who has evinced in his drefs or ftyle of living a preference to French manners, who did not lofe by it in the opinion of his countrymen.

What I have faid of French manners is applicable to foreign manners in general, which

which are all in fome degree French, and the particular differences are not diftinguifhed by the Englifh.

The fentiments of the citizens of Geneva are more analogous in many refpects to the turn of thinking in England, than to the general opinions in France. Yet a Genevois in London will univerfally pafs for a Frenchman.

An Englifh boy, fent to Geneva at an early period of life, and remaining there fix or feven years, if his parents be not along with him, will probably, in the eyes of the Englifh, appear a kind of Frenchman all his life after. This is an inconvenience which ought to be avoided with the greateft attention.

With regard to the objections againft public fchools, they are in many refpects applicable to thofe of every country. But I freely own, they never appeared to me
fufficient

sufficient to overbalance the advantages which attend that method of education; particularly as it is conducted in English public schools.

I have perceived a certain hardihood and manliness of character in boys who have had a public education, superior to what appears in those of the same age educated privately.

At a public school, though a general attention is paid to the whole, in many particulars each boy is necessitated to decide and act for himself. His reputation among his companions depends solely on his own conduct. This gradually strengthens the mind, inspires firmness and decision, and prevents that wavering imbecility observable in those who have been long accustomed to rely upon the assistance and opinion of others.

The

The original impreffions which fink into the heart and mind, and form the character, never change.—The objects of our attention vary in the different periods of life. —This is fometimes miftaken for a change of character, which in reality remains effentially the fame.—He who is referved, deceitful, cruel, or avaricious, when a boy, will not, in any future period of life, become open, faithful, compaffionate, or generous.

The young mind has, at a public fchool, the beft chance of receiving thofe fentiments which incline the heart to friendfhip, and correct felfifhnefs. They are drawn in by obfervation, which is infinitely more powerful than precept.

A boy perceives, that courage, generofity, gratitude, command the efteem and applaufe of all his companions. He cherifhes thefe qualities in his own breaft, and endeavours to connect himfelf in friendfhip with thofe who poffefs them.—He fees that meannefs of fpirit, ingratitude, and perfidy, are the objects of deteftation.—He fhuns the boys who difplay any indications of thefe odious qualities. What is the object of contempt or applaufe to his fchoolfellows he will endeavour to graft into, or eradicate from, his own character, with ten thoufand times more eagernefs than that which was applauded and cenfured by his tutor or parents.

The admonitions of thefe laft have probably loft their effect by frequent repetition; or he may imagine their maxims are only applicable to a former age, and to manners which are obfolete.—But he feels the fentiments of his companions affect his reputation and fame in the moft fenfible manner.

In all the countries of Europe, England excepted, fuch a deference is paid to boys of rank at the public fchools, that emulation,

tion, the chief spur to diligence, is greatly blunted.—The boys in the middle rank of life are depressed by the insolence of their titled companions, which they are not allowed to correct or retaliate.——This has the worst effect on the minds of both, by rendering these more insolent, and those more abject.

The public schools in England disdain this mean partiality; and are, on that account, peculiarly useful to boys of high rank and great fortune. These young people are exceedingly apt to imbibe false ideas of their own importance, which in those impartial seminaries will be perfectly ascertained, and the real merit of the youths weighed in juster scales than are generally to be found in a parent's house.

The young peer will be taught by the masters, and still more effectually by his comrades, this most useful of all lessons,—

to expect diſtinction and eſteem from perſonal qualities only; becauſe no other can make him eſtimable, or even ſave him from contempt.——He will ſee a dunce of high rank flogged with as little ceremony as the ſon 'of a tailor; and the richeſt coward kicked about by his companions equally with the pooreſt poltroon.—He will find that diligence, genius, and ſpirit, are the true ſources of ſuperiority and applauſe, both within and without the ſchool.

The active principle of emulation, when allowed full play, as in the chief ſchools in England, operates in various ways, and always with a good effect.——If a boy finds that he falls beneath his companions in literary merit, he will endeavour to excel them in intrepidity, or ſome other accompliſhment.——If he be brought to diſgrace for neglecting his exerciſe, he will try to ſave himſelf from contempt by the firmneſs with which he bears his puniſhment.

The

The liftleffnefs and indolence to be found fo frequently among our young people of rank, are not to be imputed to their education at a public fchool, which in reality has the greateft tendency to counteract thefe habits, and often does fo, and gives an energy to the mind which remains through life.

Thofe wretched qualities creep on afterwards, when the youths become their own mafters, and have enfeebled their minds by indulging in all the pleafures which fortune puts in their power, and luxury prefents.

Upon the whole, I am clearly of opinion, that the earlieft period of every Englifhman's education, during which the mind receives the moft lafting impreffions, ought to be in England.

If, however, the opinion of relations, or any peculiarity in fituation, prevents his being

being educated at home, Geneva fhould be preferred to any other place. Or if, by fome neglect, either of his own or his parents, a young Englifh gentleman of fortune has allowed the firft years of youth to fly unimproved, and has attained the age of feventeen or eighteen with little literary knowledge, I know no place where he may have a better chance of recovering what he has loft than in this city. He may have a choice of men of eminence, in every branch of literature, to affift him in his ftudies, a great proportion of whom are men of genius, and as amiable in their manners as they are eminent in their particular profeffions.

He will have conftant opportunities of being in company with very ingenious people, whofe thoughts and converfation turn upon literary fubjects. In fuch fociety, a young man will feel the neceffity of fome degree of ftudy. This will gradually form

form a taſte for knowledge, which may remain through life.'

It may alſo be numbered among the advantages of this place, that there are few objects of diſſipation, and hardly any ſources of amuſement, beſides thoſe derived from the natural beauties of the country, and from an intimacy with a people by whoſe converſation a young man can ſcarce fail to improve.

P. S. An Engliſh nobleman and his lady having taken the reſolution of educating their ſon at Geneva, attended him hither, and have effectually prevented the inconveniencies above mentioned, by remaining with him for ſeven or eight years.

The hoſpitality, generoſity, and benevolent diſpoſitions of this family had acquired them the higheſt degree of popularity. I ſaw them leave the place. Their carriage could with difficulty move through the multitude,

multitude, who were affembled in the ftreets.——Numbers of the poorer fort, who had been relieved by their fecret charity, unable longer to obey the injunctions of their benefactors, proclaimed their gratitude aloud.

The young gentleman was obliged to come out again and again to his old friends and companions, who preffed around the coach to bid him farewel, and exprefs their forrow for his departure, and their wifhes for his profperity. The eyes of the parents overflowed with tears of happinefs; and the whole family carried along with them the affections of the greater part, and the efteem of all the citizens.

LETTER XXXII.

Geneva.

SUICIDE is very frequent at Geneva. I am told this has been the cafe ever fince the oldeſt people in the republic can remember; and there is reaſon to believe, that it happens oftener here, in proportion to the number of inhabitants, than in England, or any other country of Europe.

The multiplicity of inſtances which has occurred fince I have been here is aſtoniſhing. Two that have happened very lately are remarkable for the peculiar circumſtances which accompanied them.

'The firſt was occaſioned by a ſudden and unaccountable fit of deſpair, which ſeized the ſon of one of the wealthieſt and moſt reſpectable

respectable citizens of the republic. This young gentleman had, in appearance, every reason to be satisfied with his lot. He was handsome, and in the vigour of youth, married to a woman of an excellent character, who had brought him a great fortune, and by whom he was the father of a fine child. In the midst of all these blessings, surrounded by every thing which could inspire a man with an attachment to life, he felt it insupportable, and without any obvious cause of chagrin, determined to destroy himself.

Having passed some hours with his mother, a most valuable woman, and with his wife and child, he left them in apparent good-humour, went into another room, applied the muzzle of a musket to his forehead, thrust back the trigger with his toe, and blew out his brains, in the hearing of the unsuspecting company he had just quitted.

The

The fecond inftance, is that of a blackfmith, who, taking the fame fatal refolution, and not having any convenient inftrument at hand, charged an old gun-barrel with a brace of bullets, and putting one end into the fire of his forge, tied a ftring to the handle of the bellows, by pulling of which he could make them play, while he was at a convenient diftance. Kneeling down, he then placed his head near the mouth of the barrel, and moving the bellows by means of the ftring, they blew up the fire, he keeping his head with aftonifhing firmnefs, and horrible deliberation, in that pofition, till the farther end of the barrel was fo heated as to kindle the powder, whofe explofion inftantly drove the bullets through his brains.

Though I know that this happened literally as I have related, yet there is fomething fo extraordinary, and almoft incredible, in the circumftances, that perhaps
I fhould

I fhould not have mentioned it, had it not been well attefted, and known to the inhabitants of Geneva, and all the Englifh who are at prefent here.

Why fuicide is more frequent in Great Britain and Geneva than elfewhere, would be a matter of curious inveftigation. For it appears very extraordinary, that men fhould be moft inclined to kill themfelves in countries where the bleffings of life are beft fecured. There muft be fome ftrong and peculiar caufe for an effect fo prepofterous.

Before coming here, I was of opinion, that the frequency of fuicide in England was occafioned in a great meafure by the ftormy and unequal climate, which, while it clouds the fky, throws alfo a gloom over the minds of the natives.—To this caufe, foreigners generally add, that of the ufe of coal, inftead of wood, for fuel.

I refted

I rested satisfied with some vague theory, built on these taken together:—But neither can account for the same effect at Geneva, where coal is not used, and where the climate is the same with that in Switzerland, Savoy, and the neighbouring parts of France, where instances of suicide are certainly much more rare.

Without presuming to decide what are the remote causes of this fatal propensity, it appears evident to me, that no reasoning can have the smallest force in preventing it, but what is founded upon the soul's immortality and a future state.—What effect can the common arguments have on a man who does not believe that necessary and important doctrine?—He may be told, that he did not give himself life, therefore he has no right to take it away;—that he is a centinel on a post, and ought to remain till he is relieved;——what is all this to the

man who thinks he is never to be queftioned for his violence and defertion?

If you attempt to pique this man's pride, by afferting, that it is a greater proof of courage to bear the ills of life, than to flee from them; he will anfwer you from the Roman hiftory, and afk, Whether Cato, Caffius, and Marcus Brutus, were cowards?

The great legiflator of the Jews feems to have been convinced, that no law or argument againft fuicide could have any influence on the minds of people who were ignorant of the foul's immortality; and therefore, as he did not think it neceffary to inftruct them in the one (for reafons which the Bifhop of Gloucefter has un-folded in his treatife on the Divine Legation of Mofes), he alfo thought it fuperfluous to give them any exprefs law againft the other.

Thofe

Thofe philofophers, therefore, who have endeavoured to fhake this great and important conviction from the minds of men, have thereby opened a door to fuicide as well as to other crimes.—For, whoever reafons againft that, without founding upon the doctrine of a future ftate, will foon fee all his arguments overturned.

It muft be acknowledged, indeed, that in many cafes this queftion is decided by men's feelings, independent of reafonings of any kind.

Nature has not trufted a matter of fo great importance entirely to the fallible reafon of man; but has planted in the human breaft fuch a love of life, and horror of death, as feldom can be overcome even by the greateft misfortunes.

But there is a difeafe which fometimes affects the body, and afterwards communicates its baneful influence to the mind, over which

which it hangs such a cloud of horrors as renders life absolutely insupportable. In this dreadful state, every pleasing idea is banished, and all the sources of comfort in life are poisoned.——Neither fortune, honours, friends, nor family, can afford the smallest satisfaction.——Hope, the last pillar of the wretched, falls to the ground— Despair lays hold of the abandoned sufferer —Then all reasoning becomes vain—— Even arguments of religion have no weight, and the poor creature embraces death as his only friend, which, as he thinks, may terminate, but cannot augment, his misery.

I am, &c.

P. S. You need not write till you hear from me again, as I think it is probable that we shall have left this place before your letter could arrive.

LETTER XXXIII.

Laufanne.

THE D— of H—— having a defire to vifit fome of the German Courts, we bade adieu to our friends at Geneva, and are thus far on our intended journey. It is of peculiar advantage in Germany, above all other countries, to be in company with a man of rank and high title, becaufe it facilitates your reception every where, and fuperfedes the neceffity of recommendatory letters.

I have met here with my friend B—n, whofe company and converfation have retarded our journey, by fupplying the chief objects of travelling, if amufement and inftruction are to be ranked among them. He is here with the M——s of L——y, a lively, a lively, spirited young man;—one of those easy, careless characters, so much beloved by their intimates, and so regardless of the opinion of the rest of mankind.

Since you hold me to my promise of writing so very regularly, you must sometimes expect to receive a letter dated from three or four different places, when either my short stay in one place deprives me of the leisure, or meeting with nothing uncommon in another deprives me of materials for so long a letter as you require.

The road from Geneva to this town is along the side of the lake, through a delightful country, abounding in vineyards, which produce the *vin de la cote*, so much esteemed. All the little towns on the way, Nyon, Rolle, and Morges, are finely situated, neatly built, and inhabited by a thriving and contented people.

Lausanne

Lauſanne is the capital of this charming country, which formerly belonged to the Duke of Savoy, but is now under the dominion of the canton of Bern.

However mortifying this may be to the former poſſeſſor, it has certainly been a happy diſpenſation to the inhabitants of the Pays de Vaud, who are in every reſpect more at their eaſe, and in a better ſituation, than any of the ſubjects of his Sardinian Majeſty.

This city is ſituated near the lake, and at the diſtance of about thirty miles from Geneva. As the nobility, from the country, and from ſome parts of Switzerland, and the families of ſeveral officers, who have retired from ſervice, reſide here, there is an air of more eaſe and gaiety (perhaps alſo more politeneſs) in the ſocieties at Lauſanne, than in thoſe of Geneva; at leaſt this is firmly believed and aſſerted by all the nobles of this place, who confider themfelves as greatly fuperior to the citizens of Geneva. Thefe, on the other hand, talk a good deal of the poverty, frivoloufnefs, and ignorance of thofe fame nobility, and make no fcruple of ranking their own enlightened mechanics above them in every effential quality.

Vevay.

The road between Laufanne and Vevay is very mountainous; but the mountains are cultivated to the fummits, and covered with vines.——This would have been impracticable on account of the fteepnefs, had not the proprietors built ftrong ftone-walls at proper intervals, one above the other, which fupport the foil, and form little terraffes from the bottom to the top of the mountains.

The

The peasants ascend by narrow stairs, and, before they arrive at the ground they are to cultivate, have frequently to mount higher than a mason who is employed in repairing the top of a steeple.

The mountainous nature of this country subjects it to frequent torrents, which, when violent, sweep away vines, soil, and walls in one common destruction. The inhabitants behold the havoc with a steady concern, and, without giving way to the clamorous rage of the French, or sinking into the gloomy despair of the English, think only of the most effectual means of repairing the loss.—As soon as the storm has abated, they begin, with admirable patience and perseverance, to rebuild the walls, to carry fresh earth on hurdles to the top of the mountain, and to spread a new soil wherever the old has been washed away.

Where

Where property is perfectly secure, and men allowed to enjoy the fruits of their own labour, they are capable of efforts unknown in those countries where despotism renders every thing precarious, and where a tyrant reaps what slaves have sown.

This part of the Pays de Vaud is inhabited by the descendents of those unhappy people, who were driven by the most absurd and cruel persecution from the vallies of Piedmont and Savoy.

I will not assert, that the iniquity of the persecutors has been visited upon their children; but the sufferings and stedfastness of the persecuted seem to be recompensed by the happy situation in which their children of the third and fourth generations are now placed.

Vevay is a pretty little town, containing between three and four thousand inhabitants.

ants. It is fweetly fituated on a plain, near the head of the lake of Geneva, where the Rhone enters. The mountains behind the town, though exceedingly high, are entirely cultivated, like thofe on the road from Laufanne.

There is a large village about half-way up the mountain, in a direct line above Vevay, which, viewed from below, feems adhering to the fide of the precipice, and has a very fingular and romantic appearance.

The principal church is detached from the town, and fituated on a hill which overlooks it. From the terrace, or church-yard, there is a view of the Alps, the Rhone, the lake, with towns and villages on its margin.——Within this church the body of General Ludlow is depofited. That fteady republican withdrew from Laufanne to this place, after the affaffination of his friend Lifle, who was fhot through the heart,

heart, as he was going to church, by a ruffian, who had come acrofs the lake for that purpofe, and who, amidft the confufion occafioned by the murder, got fafe to the boat, and efcaped to the Duke of Savoy's territories on the other fide, where he was openly protected.—This was a pitiful way of avenging the death of a monarch, who, whether juftly or not, had been publicly condemned and executed.

There is a long Latin epitaph on Ludlow's monument, enumerating many circumftances of his life, but omitting the moft remarkable of them all. He is called, Patriæ libertatis defenfor, et poteftatis arbitrariæ propugnator acerrimus, &c.—But no nearer hint is given of his having been one of King Charles the Firft's judges, and of his having figned the fentence againft that ill-fated Prince.

However fond the Swifs in general may be of liberty, and however partial to its
assertors,

assertors, it is presumable that those who protected Ludlow, did not approve of this part of his story, and on that account a particular mention of it was not made on his tomb.

There is no travelling by post through Switzerland; we therefore hired horses at Geneva, to carry us to Basil; from whence we can proceed by post to Strasbourg, which is the route we design to take. We leave Lausanne the day after to-morrow.

LETTER XXXIV.

Bern.

ON my return from Vevay to Laufanne, I found our friend, Mr. H——y, at the inn, with the D— of H——. His Grace inclines to remain fome time longer at that city; but defired that I might proceed with the carriages and all the fervants, except his valet-de-chambre and one footman, to Strafbourg, which I readily agreed to, on his promifing to join me there within a few days. H—y, at the fame time, made the very agreeable propofal of accompanying me to Strafbourg, where he will remain till our departure from thence, leaving his chaife for the D—.

We began our journey the following day, and were efcorted as far as Payerne by
Meffrs.

Messrs. B——n and O——n, where we passed a gay evening, and proceeded next morning to the town of Avanche, the capital of Switzerland in Tacitus's time*.

No country in the world can be more agreeable to travellers during the summer than Switzerland: For, besides the commodious roads and comfortable inns, some of the most beautiful objects of nature, woods, mountains, lakes, intermingled with fertile fields, vineyards, and scenes of the most perfect cultivation, are here presented to the eye in greater variety, and on a larger scale, than in any other country.

From Avanche we advanced to Murten, or Murat, as it is pronounced by the

---

* Near this town the Helvetians were defeated by Cæcina, one of Vitellius's Lieutenants.—Multa hominum millia cæsa, multa sub corona venumdata, Cumque direptis omnibus, Aventicum gentis caput justo agmine peteretur.

Taciti Historia, lib. i. cap. 68.

French,

French, a neat little town, fituated upon a rifing ground, on the fide of the lake of the fame name.

The army of Charles Duke of Burgundy, befieging this town, was defeated, with great flaughter, by the Swifs, in the year 1476. Near the road, within a mile of Murat, there is a little building full of human bones, which are faid to be thofe of the Burgundians flain in that battle. As this curious cabinet was erected many years after the battle, it may be fuppofed, that fome of the bones of the victors are here packed up along with thofe of the vanquifhed, in order to fwell the collection.

There are feveral infcriptions on the chapel.

DEO OPTIM. MAX.
CAROLI INCLITI ET FORTISSIMI BURGUNDIÆ DUCIS
EXERCITUS MURATUM OBSIDENS AB HELVETIIS
CÆSUS HOC SUI MONUMENTUM RELIQUIT, 1476.

On another fide is the following:

SACELLUM
QUO RELIQUIAS
EXERCITUS BURGUNDICI
AB HELVETIIS, A. 1476,
PIA ANTIQUITAS CONDIDIT.
RENOVARI
VIISQUE PUBLICIS MUNIRI
JUSSERUNT
RERUM NUNC DOMINÆ
RE!PUBLICÆ
BERNENSIS ET FRIBURGENSIS
ANNO 1755.

The borders of the lake of Murat are enriched with gentlemen's houfes, and villages in great abundance.

The drefs, manners, and perfons of the inhabitants of this country indicate a different people from the Genevois, Savoyards, or the inhabitants of the Pays de Vaud.

We dined at Murat, and remained several hours in the town. There was a fair, and a great concourse of people.——The Swifs peasants are the tallest and most robust I have ever seen. Their dress is very particular.—They have little round hats, like those worn by the Dutch skippers.—Their coats and waistcoats are all of a kind of coarse black cloth.—Their breeches are made of coarse linen, something like sailors trowsers; but drawn together in plaits below the knees, and the stockings are of the same stuff with the breeches.

The women wear short jackets, with a great superfluity of buttons. The unmarried women value themselves on the length of their hair, which they separate into two divisions, and allow to hang at its full length, braided with ribands in the Ramillie fashion.——After marriage, these tresses are no longer permitted to hang down;

down; but, being twisted round the head in spiral lines, are fixed at the crown with large silver pins. This is the only difference in point of dress which matrimony makes.

Married and unmarried wear straw hats, ornamented with black ribands. So far the women's dress is becoming enough; but they have an aukward manner of fixing their petticoats so high as to leave hardly any waist. This encroachment of the petticoats upon the waist, with the amazing number they wear, gives a size and importance to the lower and hind part of the body to which it is by no means entitled, and mightily deforms the appearance of the whole person.

The elegant figure of the Venus de Medicis, or of the D———ss of D———re, would be impaired, or annihilated, under such a preposterous load of dress.———As we arrived only this afternoon, I can say nothing of Bern. You shall hear more in my next. Meanwhile, I am, &c.

LETTER XXXV.

Bern.

BERN is a regular well-built town, with some air of magnificence. The houses are of a fine, white, free-stone, and pretty uniform, particularly in the principal street, where they are all exactly of the same height. There are piazzas on each side, with a walk, raised four feet above the level of the street, very commodious in wet weather.

A small branch of the Aar has been turned into this street, and being confined to a narrow channel in the middle, which has a considerable slope, it runs with great rapidity; and, without being a disagreeable object of itself, is of great service in keeping the street clean.

Another

Another circumstance contributes to render this one of the most cleanly towns in Europe:—Criminals are employed in removing rubbish from the streets and public walks. The more atrocious delinquents are chained to waggons, while those who are condemned for smaller crimes, are employed in sweeping the light rubbish into the rivulet, and throwing the heavier into the carts or waggons, which their more criminal companions are obliged to push or draw along.

These wretches have collars of iron fixed around their necks, with a projecting handle in the form of a hook to each, by which, on the slightest offence or mutiny, they may be seized, and are entirely at the command of the guard, whose duty it is to see them perform their work.—People of both sexes are condemned to this labour for months, years, or for life, according to the nature of their crimes.

It is alleged, that over and above the deterring from crimes, which is effected by this, in common with the other methods of punishing, there is the additional advantage, of obliging the criminal to repair by his labour the injury which he has done to the community.

I suspect, however, that this advantage is overbalanced by the bad effects of habituating people to behold the misery of their fellow-creatures, which I imagine gradually hardens the hearts of the spectators, and renders them less susceptible of the emotions of compassion and pity;—feelings, which, perhaps of all others, have the best influence upon, and are the most becoming, human nature. Juvenal says,

———————————— mollissima corda
Humano generi dare se natura fatetur,
Quæ lachrymas dedit: hæc nostri pars optima sensûs.

Wherever public executions and punishments are frequent, the common people have been observed to acquire a greater degree of insensibility, and cruelty of disposition, than in places where such scenes seldom occur.—I remember, while I was at Geneva, where executions are very rare, a young man was condemned to be hanged for murder, and there was a general gloom and uneasiness evident in every society for several days before and after the execution.

The public buildings at Bern, as the hospital, the granary, the guard-house, the arsenal, and the churches, are magnificent. There is a very elegant building just completed, with accommodations for many public amusements, such as balls, concerts, and theatrical entertainments. There are also apartments for private societies and assemblies. It was built by a voluntary subscription among the nobility; and no societies, but of the patrician order, are allowed there.

Theatrical entertainments are seldom permitted at Bern; none have as yet been performed at this new theatre.

The walk by the great church was formerly the only public walk, and much admired on account of the view from it, and the peculiarity of its situation, being on a level with the streets on one side, and some hundred feet of perpendicular height above them on the other. But there is now another public walk, at some distance without the town, which has been lately made upon a high bank by the side of the Aar, and is the most magnificent I ever saw belonging to this or any other town. From it there is a commanding view of the river, the town of Bern, the country about it, and the Glaciers of Switzerland.

I have

I have vifited the library, where, befides the books, there are a few antiques, and fome other curiofities. The fmall figure of the prieft pouring wine between the horns of a bull, is valuable only becaufe it illuftrates a paffage in Virgil, and has been mentioned by Addifon.

An addition was lately made to this library by a collection of Englifh books, magnificently bound, which were fent as a prefent by an Englifh gentleman; who, though he has thought proper to conceal his name, has fufficiently difcovered his political principles by the nature of the collection, amongft which, I diftinguifhed Milton's works, particularly his profe writings; Algernon Sidney on Government, Locke, Ludlow's Memoirs, Gordon's tranflation of Tacitus, Addifon's works, particularly The Freeholder; Marvel's works, Steel's, &c. They were the largeft and fineft editions, and might be about the value of of 200 l.—This gentleman made a prefent of the fame nature to the public library at Geneva.

I happened to open the Glafgow edition of Homer, which I faw here, on a blank page of which was an addrefs in Latin to the Corfican General, Paoli, figned James Bofwell. This very elegant book had been fent, I fuppofe, as a prefent from Mr. Bofwell to his friend the General; and, when that unfortunate chief was obliged to abandon his country, has, with others of his effects, fallen into the hands of the Swifs officer in the French fervice, who made a prefent of the Homer to this library.

The arfenal I could not have omitted feeing had I been fo inclined, as the Bernois value themfelves on the trophies contained in it, and upon the quantity, good condition, and arrangement of the arms.

Nothing

Nothing interefted me fo much as the figures of the brave Switzers, who firft took arms againft tyranny, and that of William Tell, who is reprefented aiming at the apple on his fon's head. I contemplated this with an emotion which was created by the circumftances of the ftory, not by the workmanfhip; for, at that moment, I fhould have beheld with neglect the moft exquifite ftatue that ever was formed of Auguftus Cæfar.

Surely no characters have fo juft a claim to the admiration and gratitude of pofterity as thofe who have freed their countrymen from the capricious infolence of tyrants: And whether all the incidents of Tell's ftory be true or fabulous, the men (whoever they were) who roufed and incited their fellow-citizens to throw off the Auftrian yoke, deferve to be regarded as patriots, having undoubtedly been actuated

by

by that principle, fo dear to every generous heart, the fpirit of independence.

> " Who with the gen'rous ruftics fate,
> " On Uri's rock, in clofe divan,
> " And wing'd that arrow fure as fate,
> " Which afcertain'd the facred rights of
> " man."

Mr. Addifon obferves, that there is no great pleafure in vifiting arfenals, merely to fee a repetition of thefe magazines of war; yet it is worth while, as it gives an idea of the force of a ftate, and ferves to fix in the mind the moft confiderable parts of its hiftory.

The arms taken from the Burgundians, in the various battles which eftablifhed the liberty of Switzerland, are difplayed here; alfo the figure of the General of Bern, who, in the year 1536, conquered the Pays de Vaud from Charles III. Duke of Savoy:—And, if they have no trophies to fhew of a later date, I am convinced it is becaufe they

they are too poor and too wife to aim at any extenfion of dominion:—And becaufe all the neighbouring powers are at length become fenfible, that the nature of their country, and their perfonal valour, have rendered the Swifs as unconquerable, as, from political confiderations, they are averfe to attempt conquefts.

LETTER XXXVI.

Bern.

THE different cantons of Switzerland, though united together by a common bond, and all of a republican form of government, differ in the nature of that form, as well as in religion.

The Roman Catholic religion being favourable to monarchy, one would naturally imagine, that, when adopted by a republic, it would gradually wind up the government to the higheſt pitch of ariſtocracy.

The fact neverthelefs is, that thoſe cantons, which are in the ſtrongeſt degree democratical, are of the Popiſh perſuaſion; and the moſt perfect ariſtocracy of them all

all is established in this Protestant canton of Bern, which is also indeed the most powerful. In extent of country, and number of inhabitants, it is reckoned nearly equal to all the others taken together.

The nobility of Bern are accused of an extraordinary degree of pride and stateliness. They affect to keep the citizens at a great distance; and it is with difficulty that their wives and daughters will condescend to mix with the mercantile families at balls, assemblies, and such public occasions, where numbers seem essential to the nature of the entertainment; by which means a nobility ball loses in cheerfulness what it retains in dignity, and is often, as I am told, as devoid of amusement as it is solemn.

The whole power of the government, and all the honourable offices of the state, are in the hands of the nobility. As it is not permitted

permitted them to trade, they would naturally fall into poverty without this resource: But by the number of places which the nobles enjoy, and to which very considerable pensions are annexed, the poorest of them are enabled to support their families with dignity.

The bailliages, into which the whole canton and the conquered territories are divided, form lucrative and honourable establishments for the principal families of Bern. The bailiff is governor and judge in his own district, and there is a magnificent chateau in each for his accommodation. An appeal may be made from all subordinate courts to him; as also from his decision, to the council at Bern.

The nobility of Bern, though born to be judges, are not always instructed in law. It has therefore been thought requisite, to appoint a certain number of persons, as their assessors, affeffors, who have been bred to the profeffion. But in cafe the judge fhould differ from thofe affeffors, and retain his own opinion in fpite of their remonftrances, as nobility has the precedency of law, the decifion muft be given according to the will of the judge.

This office remains in the hands of the fame perfon for the term of fix years only. I have been informed, that in fome of thefe bailliages, the governor may live with proper magnificence, and lay up, during the period of his office, two or three thoufand pounds, without extortion, or unbecoming parfimony. There is no law againft his being afterwards named to another bailliage.

The executive power of the government, with all the lucrative and honourable offices, being thus in the hands of the nobility, it may be imagined, that the middle and lower ranks of people are poor and oppreffed.

preſſed. This, however, is by no means the caſe; for the citizens, I mean the merchants and trades-people, ſeem, in general, to enjoy all the comforts and conveniencies of life. And the peaſantry is uncommonly wealthy throughout the whole canton of Bern.

The Swiſs have no objection to their nobles being their judges, and to the principal offices of government remaining in their hands. They look upon the nobility as their natural ſuperiors, and think, that they and their families ought to be ſupported with a certain degree of ſplendor:— But the power of direct taxation is a different queſtion, and muſt be managed with all poſſible caution and delicacy.—It is a common cauſe, and the conduct of the nobles in this particular is watched with very jealous eyes. They are ſufficiently aware of this, and uſe their power with moderation. But leſt the nobles ſhould at any time forget, a very good hint is given in a German inscription in the arsenal, implying, That the insolence and rapacity of high rank had brought about the liberty of Switzerland.

A people who have always arms in their hands, and form the only military force of the country, are in no danger of being oppressed and irritated with taxes.

It has been considered by some as a pernicious policy in the Swiss, to allow so many of their inhabitants to serve as mercenaries in the different armies of Europe. There are others, who consider this measure as expedient, or less pernicious in the Swiss cantons, than it would be in any other country.

They who support this opinion, assert, that every part of Switzerland, which is capable of cultivation, is already improved to the highest degree;—that, after retaining a sufficient number of hands to keep it always in this condition, and for the support of every manufactory, still there remains a surplus of inhabitants, which forms the troops that are allowed to go into foreign services. They add, that these troops only engage for a limited number of years, after the expiration of which, many of them return, with money, to their native country; and all of them, by stipulation, may be recalled by the state on any emergency.—By this means, they retain a numerous and well-disciplined army on foot; which, so far from being a burden, in reality enriches the state;—an advantage which no other people ever possessed.

There is still another motive for this measure, which, though it be not openly avowed, yet, I suspect, has considerable weight: The council are perhaps afraid, that if the young nobility were kept at home,

home, where they could have but few objects to occupy them, they might cabal and spread diffentions in the ftate; or perhaps, through idlenefs and ambition, excite dangerous infurrections among the peafants. For, although the laws are fevere againft ftate crimes, and eafily put in execution againft ordinary offenders, it might be difficult and dangerous to punifh a popular young nobleman.

It may on thefe accounts be thought highly prudent, to allow a large proportion of them to exhauft, in fome foreign fervice, the fiery and reftlefs years of youth, which at home might have been fpent in faction and dangerous intrigues. Very probably the ftates would incline to permit the officers to go, while they retained the private men at home; but are under a neceffity of allowing the latter alfo, becaufe without them the officers could not be raifed to thofe diftinguifhed fituations in foreign

foreign fervices which are their greateft inducements to leave their own country.

After having ferved a certain time, almoft all of them return to Switzerland. Some, becaufe they are tired of diffipation; others to inherit a paternal eftate; and many with penfions from the Princes they have ferved.—The heat of youth is then moft probably over.—They begin to afpire to thofe offices in their own country to which their birth gives them a claim, and which they now prefer to the luftre of military rank. They wifh to fupport thofe laws, and that government, which they find fo partial to their families; or they defire to pafs the remainder of life in eafe and retirement on their paternal eftates.

It is remarkable, that the Swifs officers, who return from foreign fervices, particularly that of France, inftead of importing French manners to their native mountains, and infecting their countrymen with the luxuries and fopperies of that nation, throw off all foreign airs with their uniform, and immediately refume the plain and frugal ftyle of life which prevails in their own country.

LETTER XXXVII.

Basil.

HAVING, on a former occasion, made a more extensive tour through Switzerland, we determined not to deviate from the direct road to Strasbourg. In pursuance of this resolution, H―――y and I, when we left Bern, passed by Soleurre, the capital of the canton of the same name.

Soleurre is an agreeable little town situated on the river Aar. The houses are neatly built, and not inelegant; the meanest of them have a cleanly appearance. The common people seem to be in easier circumstances, and have a greater air of content, than in any Roman Catholic country I have ever visited. The inn where we lodged

lodged has the comfortable look of an English one. The French ambaffador to the
cantons has his refidence in this town. One
of the churches of Soleurre is the moft magnificent modern building in Switzerland.

The arfenal is ftored with arms in proportion to the number of inhabitants in the
canton; and there are trophies, and other
monuments of the valour of their anceftors,
as in the arfenal of Bern. In the middle
of the hall there are thirteen figures of men
in complete armour, reprefenting the thirteen Swifs cantons.

The country between Soleurre and Bafil,
though very hilly, is beautiful, perhaps
the more fo on that account; becaufe of
the variety of furface and different views it
prefents. H——y and I had more leifure
to admire thofe fine landfcapes than we
wifhed, for the axle-tree of the chaife
broke at fome miles diftant from Bafil.

It

It was the gay feafon of the vintage.—
The country was crowded with peafantry
of both fexes and every age, all employed
in gathering and carrying home the grapes.
Our walk for thefe few miles was agreeable
and amufing. In all countries this is the
feafon of joy and feftivity, and approaches
neareft the exaggerated defcription which
the ancient poets have given of rural happinefs. Perhaps there is in reality not fo
much exaggeration in their defcription, as
alteration in our manners.—For, if the peafants were allowed to enjoy the fruits of
their own labour, would not their lives be
more delightful than thofe of any other
people?—In fpite of poverty and oppreffion,
a happy enthufiafm, a charming madnefs,
and perfect oblivion of care, are diffufed
all over France during the vintage.—Every
village is enlivened with mufic, dancing, and
glee;—and were it not for their tattered
cloaths and emaciated countenances, one
who viewed them in the vintage feafon,
would

would imagine the country people of France in a situation as enviable as that which, according to the Poets, was formerly enjoyed by the Shepherds of Arcadia.—The peasantry of this country have not so great a sensibility or expression of joy; and though blessed with health, freedom, and abundance, a composed satisfaction, a kind of phlegmatic good-humour, mark the boundaries of their happiness.

When we arrived at Basil, we went directly to the Three Kings. This inn, in point of situation, is the most agreeable you can well imagine. The Rhone washes its walls, and the windows of a large dining-room look across that noble river to the fertile plains on the opposite side.

I am just returned from that same dining-room, where H———y and I thought proper to sup.—There were ten or a dozen people at table.—I sat next to a genteel-looking

looking man from Strasbourg, with whom I converfed a good deal during fupper. He had for his companion a round-faced, rofy, plump gentleman from Amfterdam, who did not fpeak French; but the Strafburgher addreffed him from time to time in Low Dutch, to which the other replied by nods.

When the retreat of the greater part of the company had contracted the little circle which remained, I expreffed fome regret to my Strafbourg acquaintance, that Mr. H—y and I could not fpeak a little Dutch; or that his friend could not fpeak French, that we might enjoy the pleafure of his converfation. This was immediately tranflated to the Dutchman, who heard it with great compofure, and then took his pipe from his mouth, and made an anfwer, which I got our interpreter, with fome difficulty, to explain. It was to this effect:—That we ought to confole ourfelves for the accident of our not underftanding each other; for as

we

we had no connection, or dealings in trade together, our conversing could not possibly answer any useful purpose. H——y made a low bow to this compliment, saying, that the justness and good sense of that remark had certainly escaped my observation, as he acknowledged it had hitherto done his.

A man that travels, you see, my friend, and takes care to get into good company, is always learning something.—Had I not visited the Three Kings at Basil, I might have conversed all my lifetime without knowing the true use of language.

LETTER XXXVIII.

Bafil.

THERE has been an interval of three days fince I had the converfation with my ingenious acquaintance from Amfterdam. We are affured that the chaife, which has been accommodated with a new axle-tree, will be ready this afternoon. In the interim, I fhall write you a few remarks on this town.

Bafil is larger than any town in Switzerland, but not fo populous for its fize as Geneva. The inhabitants feem to be uncommonly afraid of thieves, moft of the windows being guarded by iron bars or grates, like thofe of convents or prifons.

I obferved

I obferved at the lower end of many windows a kind of wooden box, projecting towards the ftreet, with a round glafs, of about half a foot diameter, in the middle. I was told this was for the conveniency of people within; who, without being feen, choofe to fit at the windows, and amufe themfelves by looking at the paffengers;—that they were moftly occupied by the ladies, who are taught to think it indecent to appear at the windows.

The inhabitants of Bafil feem to be of a referved and faturnine difpofition; whether it is natural or affected I cannot tell, but the few I converfed with, had fomething uncommonly ferious and formal in their manner. How an unremitting gravity and folemnity of manner in the common affairs of life, comes to be confidered as an indication of wifdom, or of extraordinary parts, is what I never could underftand.

ſtand.—So many ridiculous things occur every day in this world, that men who are endowed with that degree of ſenſibility which uſually accompanies genius, find it very difficult to maintain a continued gravity. This difficulty is abundantly felt even in the grave and learned profeſſions of law, phyſic, and divinity; and the individuals who have been moſt ſuccefsful in ſurmounting it, and who never deviate from the ſolemnity of eſtabliſhed forms, have not always been the moſt diſtinguiſhed for real knowledge or genius; though they generally are moſt admired by the multitude, who are very apt to miſtake that gravity for wiſdom, which proceeds from a literal weight of brain, and muddineſs of underſtanding. Miſtakes of the ſame kind are frequently made in forming a judgment of books, as well as men. Thoſe which profeſs a formal deſign to inſtruct and reform, and carry on the work methodically till the reader is lulled into repose, have passed for deep and useful performances; while others, replete with original observation and real instruction, have been treated as frivolous, because they are written in a familiar style, and the precepts conveyed in a sprightly and indirect manner.

Works which are composed with the laborious desire of being thought profound, have so very often the misfortune to be dull, that some people have considered the two terms as synonymous; and the men who receive it as a rule, that one set of books are profound because they are dull, may naturally conclude that others are superficial because they are entertaining. With respect to books, however, matters are soon set to rights; those of puffed and false pretensions die neglected, while those of real merit live and flourish. But with regard to the men, the catastrophe is often different; we daily see formal assuming blockheads

blockheads flourish and enjoy the fruits of their pompous impositions, while many men of talents who disdain such arts, live in obscurity, and die neglected.——I ask you pardon; I have just recollected that I was giving you some account of Basil.

The library here is much esteemed.— It is reckoned particularly rich in manuscripts. They showed us one of a Greek New Testament, with which you may believe H—y and I were greatly edified. We are told it is above a thousand years old.

At the arsenal is shown, the armour in which Charles Duke of Burgundy was killed. That unfortunate prince has ornamented all the arsenals in Switzerland with trophies.

We visited the hall where the famous Council sat so many years, and voted so intrepidly againſt the Pope. Not ſatisfied with condemning his conduct, they actually damned him in effigy. A famous painting, in the town-houſe, is ſuppoſed to have been executed under their auſpices. In this piece the Devil is repreſented driving the Pope and ſeveral eccleſiaſtics before him to Hell.—Why they ſhould ſuppoſe the Devil ſhould be ſo very active. againſt his Holineſs, I know no reaſon.

Here are many pictures of Hans Holben's (who was a native of Baſil, and the favourite painter of Henry VIII. to whom he was firſt recommended by Eraſmus); particularly, ſeveral portraits of Eraſmus, and one ſketch of Sir Thomas More's family. Though portraits are in general the moſt inſipid of all kinds of paintings, yet thoſe of ſuch celebrated perſons, done by ſuch a painter, are certainly very intereſting pieces.

The

The moſt admired of all Holben's works, is a ſuite of ſmall pieces in different compartments, repreſenting the paſſion and ſufferings of our Saviour. In theſe the colours remain with wonderful vivacity.

We were alſo conducted to the diſmal gallery, upon whoſe walls, what is called Holben's Death's Dance, is repreſented. The colours having been long expoſed to the air, are now quite faded, which I can ſcarce think is much to be regretted, for the plan of the piece is ſo wretched, that the fineſt execution could hardly prevent it from giving diſguſt.

A ſkeleton, which repreſents Death, leads off, in a dancing attitude, people of both ſexes, of all ages, and of every condition, from the emperor to the beggar. All of them diſplay the greateſt unwillingneſs to accompany their hideous partner, who, regardlefs of tears, expoftulations, and bribes, draws them along.

You will take notice, that there is a Death for each character, which occafions a naufeous repetition of the fame figure; and the reluctance marked by the different people who are forced to this hated minuet, is in fome accompanied with grimaces fo very ridiculous, that one cannot refrain from fmiling, which furely is not the effect the painter intended to produce.—If he did, of all the contrivances that ever were thought of to put people in good-humour, his muft be allowed the moft extraordinary.

To this piece, fuch as it is, Prior alludes in his ode to the memory of Colonel Villers.

Nor aw'd by forefight, nor mifled by chance,
Imperious Death directs his ebon lance,
Peoples great Henry's tomb, and leads up
  Holben's dance.

In

In this city all the clocks are an hour advanced. When it is but one o'clock in all the towns and villages around, it is exactly two at Bafil. This fingularity is of three or four hundred years ftanding; and what is as fingular as the cuftom itfelf, the origin of it is not known. This is plain, by their giving quite different accounts of it.

The moft popular ftory is, that, about four hundred years ago, the city was threatened with an affault by furprife. The enemy was to begin the attack when the large clock of the Tower at one end of the bridge fhould ftrike one after midnight. The artift who had the care of the clock, being informed that this was the expected fignal, caufed the clock to be altered, and it ftruck two inftead of one; fo the enemy thinking they were an hour too late, gave up the attempt; and in commemoration of this deliverance, all the clocks in

Bafil have ever fince ftruck two at one o'clock, and fo on.

In cafe this account of the matter fhould not be fatisfactory, they fhow, by way of confirmation, a head, which is placed near to this patriotic clock, with the face turned to the road by which the enemy was to have entered. This fame head lolls out its tongue every minute, in the moft infulting manner poffible. This was originally a piece of mechanical wit of the famous clock-maker's who faved the town. He framed it in derifion of the enemy, whom he had fo dexteroufly deceived. It has been repaired, renewed, and enabled to thruft out its tongue every minute, for thefe four hundred years, by the care of the magiftrates, who think fo excellent a joke cannot be too often repeated.

LETTER XXXIX.

Strafburg.

NOTHING can form a finer contraſt with the mountains of Switzerland than the plains of Alſace. From Baſil to Straſburg, is a continued, well cultivated plain, as flat almoſt as a bowling-green. We ſaw great quantities of tobacco hanging at the peaſants doors, as we came along, this herb being plentifully cultivated in theſe fields.

We have paſſed ſome days very agreeably in this town. One can ſcarcely be at a loſs for good company and amuſement, in a place where there is a numerous French garriſon. Marechal Contades reſides here at preſent, as commander of the troops, and governor of the province. He lives

in

in a magnificent manner. The English who happen to pass this way, as well as the officers of the garrison, have great reason to praise his hospitality and politeness.

After dining at his house, with several English gentlemen, he invited the company to his box at the playhouse. Voltaire's Enfant Prodigue was acted; and for the Petite Pièce, le François à Londres. Our nation is a little bantered, as you know, in the last. The eyes of the spectators were frequently turned towards the Marechal's box, to observe how we bore the raillery. We clapped heartily, and showed the most perfect good-humour. There was indeed no reason to do otherwise. The satire is genteel, and not too severe; and reparation is made for the liberties taken; for in the same piece, all manner of justice is done to the real good qualities belonging to the English national character.

An

An old French officer, who was in the next box to us, feemed uneafy, and hurt at the peals of laughter which burft from the audience at fome particular paffages: he touched my fhoulder, and affured me that no nation was more refpected in France than the Englifh;—adding, ' Hanc veniam damus, petimufque viciffim.'

It were to be wifhed that French characters, when brought on the Englifh ftage, had been always treated with as little feverity, and with equal juftice; and not fo often facrificed to the illiberal and abfurd prejudices of the vulgar.

I have feen the greater number of the regiments perform their exercife feparately, and there has been one general field-day fince I came hither. The French troops are infinitely better clothed, and in all refpects better appointed than they were during the laft war. For this reformation, I am told they

they are obliged to the Duc de Choiseul, who, though now in disgrace, still retains many friends in the army.

There are, besides the French, two German regiments in this garrison. These admit of the discipline of the cane upon every slight occasion, which is never permitted among the French troops. Notwithstanding their being so plentifully provided with those severe flappers to rouse their attention, I could not perceive that the German regiments went through their exercise with more precision or alertness than the French; and any difference would, in my opinion, be dearly purchased at the price of treating one soldier like a spaniel.

Perhaps what improves the hardy and phlegmatic German, would have a contrary effect on the more delicate and lively Frenchman; as the same severity which is requisite to train a pointer, would render a greyhound good for nothing.

After

After all, I queſtion very much whether this ſhocking cuſtom is abſolutely neceſſary in the armies of any nation; for, let our martinets ſay what they pleaſe, there is ſurely ſome difference between men and dogs.

With reſpect to the French, I am convinced that great ſeverity would break their ſpirit, and impair that fire and impetuoſity in attack, for which they have been diſtinguiſhed, and which makes French troops more formidable than any other quality they poſſeſs.

I muſt own I was highly pleaſed with the eaſy, familiar air, and appearance of good will, with which the French officers in general ſpeak to the common ſoldiers.—This, I am told, does not diminiſh the reſpect and obedience which ſoldiers owe to their ſuperiors, or that degree of ſubordination which military diſcipline exacts. On the contrary,

trary, it is afferted, that to thefe properties, which the French poffefs in common with other foldiers, they join a kind of grateful attachment and affection.

In fome fervices, the behaviour of the officers to the private foldiers is fo morofe, fevere, and unrelenting, that a man might be led to believe that one of their principal enjoyments was to render the lives of the common men as miferable as poffible.

If a certain degree of gentlenefs does no harm in the great articles of obedience and fubordination, it is furely worth while to pay fome attention to the feelings of fo large a proportion of mankind, as are by modern policy neceffitated to follow a military life. To put *their* happinefs entirely out of the queftion, in the government of the armies of which they form infinitely the major part, is rather hard treatment of creatures who are of the fame fpecies, employed in the fame

fame caufe, and expofed to the fame dangers with their officers.

When I began this, I intended to have told you a few things about Strafburg, inftead of which I have been led out of my way by French and German foldiers.—Digreffing is a trick to which I am very fubject, and rather than not be indulged in it, I would throw away my pen altogether.

The D— of H—— arrived here exactly at the time he propofed.

LETTER XL.

Strasburg.

THE cathedral of Strasburg is a very fine building, and never fails to attract the attention of strangers.

Our Gothic ancestors, like the Greeks and Romans, built for posterity. Their ideas in architecture, though different from those of the Grecian artists, were vast, sublime, and generous, far superior to the selfish snugness of modern taste, which is generally confined to one or two generations; the plans of our ancestors with a more extensive benevolence embrace distant ages. Many Gothic buildings still habitable evince this, and ought to inspire sentiments of gratitude to those who have not grudged such labour

and

and expence for the accommodation of their remote pofterity.

The number and magnitude of Gothic churches, in the different countries of Europe, form a prefumption, that the clergy were not devoid of public fpirit in thofe days; for if the powerful ecclefiaftics had then been entirely actuated by motives of felf-intereft, they would have turned the exceffive influence which they had acquired over the minds of their fellow-citizens, to purpofes more immediately advantageous to themfelves; inftead of encouraging them to raife magnificent churches for the ufe of the public, they might have preached it up as ftill more meritorious to build fine houfes and palaces for the immediate fervants and ambaffadors of God.—But we find very few ecclefiaftical palaces, in comparifon with the number of churches which ftill remain for the public conveniency. This fufficiently fhows the injuftice of thofe indifcriminating fatirifts, satirists, who assert that the clergy in all ages and countries have displayed a spirit equally proud and interested.

No species of architecture is better contrived for the dwelling of *heavenly pensive contemplation*, than the Gothic; it has a powerful tendency to fill the mind with sublime, solemn, and religious sentiments; the antiquity of the Gothic churches contributes to increase that veneration which their form and size inspire. We naturally feel a respect for a fabric into which we know that our forefathers have entered with reverence, and which has stood the assaults of many centuries, and of a thousand storms. That religious melancholy which usually possesses the mind in large Gothic churches, is however considerably counteracted by certain satirical bas reliefs with which the pillars and cornices of this church of Strasburg was originally ornamented.— The vices of monks are here exposed under the allegorical figure of hogs, affes, monkies, and foxes, which being dreffed in monkifh habits, perform the moft venerable functions of religion. And for the edification of thofe who do not comprehend allegory, a monk in the robes of his order, is engraved on the pulpit in a moft indecent pofture, with a nun lying by him.

Upon the whole, the cathedral of Strafburg is confidered by fome people as the moft impious, and by others as the merrieft Gothic church in Chriftendom. I leave you to folve the problem as you pleafe.— As for me, I am a very unconcerned paffenger.

I fay nothing of the great clock and its various movements. Though it was an object of admiration when firft conftructed, it is beheld with indifference by modern artifts.

I had the curiosity to ascend the steeple of this cathedral, which is reckoned one of the highest in Europe, its height being 574 feet. You may easily form an idea of the view from it, when I tell you it comprehends the town of Strasburg, the extensive plains of Alsace, with the Rhine flowing through them. Such views are not uncommon: They are always agreeable, but do not astonish and elevate the mind, like the wild, irregular, and sublime scenes in Switzerland.

One forenoon as I was sauntering through the streets with some of our countrymen, we were informed that the music of some of the regiments had been ordered to a particular church, where the Count de ———, son of Lewis the XVth by Madam de Pompadour, was expected to be at mass.— We all immediately went for the sake of the military music, and found a very numerous and genteel company attending. After having

having waited a confiderable time, it ftruck twelve, upon which the whole company retired, without hearing the mufic or mafs. —After mid-day the ceremony could not have been performed, although the Count had come. Something very important muft have intervened to prevent a Frenchman, and one of his character for politenefs, from attending on fuch an occafion. There was however a murmur of difapprobation for this want of attention, and the prieft was not applauded, who had hazarded the fouls of a whole churchful of people, out of complaifance to one man; for thófe who imagine that a mafs can fave fouls, muft admit that the want of it may be the caufe of damnation. Mr. H—y whifpered me, " In " England they would not have had half " the complaifance for the king himfelf, " accompanied by all his legitimate chil- " dren, that thefe people have fhewn to " this fon of a w—e."

To indemnify myself for this disappointment, I went the same afternoon with a French officer to hear a celebrated preacher. The subject of his discourse was the miserable situation of men who were under the dominion of their passions.—Do you wish for a sample of his discourse?—Here it is:

——" A slave in the galleys (cried the " preacher) is happier, and more free, than " a man under the tyranny of his passions; " for though the body of the slave is in " chains, his mind may be free.—Whereas " the wretch who is under the government " of his passions, has his mind, his very " soul, in chains.—Is his passion lust?—He " will sacrifice a faithful servant to gratify " it;—David did so.—Is it avarice?—he " will betray his master;—Judas did so.— " Is he attached to a mistress?—he will " murder a saint to please her;—Herod did " so."

As we returned from the church, the French officer, who had been for some time in a reverie, faid, Ma foi, cet homme parle avec beaucoup d'onction; je vais profiter de fon fermon.—Où eft-ce que vous allez? faid I.—Je m'en vais chez Nanette, replied he, pour me débarraffer de ma paffion dominante.

Among the curiofities of the cathedral, I ought to have mentioned two large bells, which they fhow to ftrangers. One is of brafs, and weighs ten tons; the other of filver, which they fay weighs above two.— They alfo fhow a large French horn, whofe hiftory is as follows.—About four hundred years ago, the Jews formed a confpiracy to betray the city, and with this identical horn, they intended to give the enemy notice when to begin the attack.

Is it not amazing that fuch a number of ftrange ftories have been circulated concerning thefe fame Jews?

The plot, however, was difcovered; many of the Jews were burnt alive, the reft were plundered of their money and effects, and banifhed the town. And this horn is founded twice every night from the battlements of the fteeple in gratitude for the deliverance.

The Jews, as you would expect, deny every circumftance of this ftory, except the murdering and pillaging their countrymen. They fay the whole ftory was fabricated to furnifh a pretext for thefe robberies and murders, and affert that the fteeple of Strafburg, as has been faid of the monument of London,

" Like a tall bully lifts the head and lies."

LETTER XLI.

Manheim.

ALL the advantages I might propose from the D— of H——'s company, did not prevent my regret at parting from my friend H—y, who set out for Lyons the same morning on which we left Strasburg.

Upon crossing the Rhine we entered into the territories of the Margrave of Baden Durlach, which lie along the banks of that river immediately opposite to Alsace.

At Rastade we were informed that the Margrave and his family were at Karlsruch. Rastade is the capital of this prince's dominions.—The town is but small, and not very populous:—The Margrave's palace, however, is sufficiently large.—We made only a ſhort ſtay to examine it, being impatient to get on to Karlſruch.

There is another very magnificent palace at Karlſruch, built in good taſte. It was begun many years ago, and has been lately finiſhed by the reigning prince.

The town of Karlſruch is built on a regular plan. It conſiſts of one principal ſtreet of above an Engliſh mile in length. This ſtreet is at a conſiderable diſtance in front of the palace, and in a parallel direction with it. All the other ſtreets go off at different angles from the principal one, in ſuch a manner as that whichſoever of them you enter, walking from it, the view is terminated by the front of the palace. The length of theſe ſmaller ſtreets is aſcertained, none of them being allowed to encroach on the ſpacious area, which is kept clear before the palace.

The principal ſtreet may be extended to any length, and as many additional ſtreets as they pleaſe may be built from it, all of which, according to this plan, will have the palace for a termination.

The houſes of this town are all as uniform as the ſtreets, being of an equal ſize and height; ſo that one would be led to imagine that none of the inhabitants are in any conſiderable degree richer or poorer than their neighbours. There are indeed a few new houſes, more elegant than the others, belonging to ſome of the officers of the court, built at one ſide of the palace; but they are not, properly ſpeaking, in the town.

Having announced in the uſual form, that we wiſhed to have the honour of paying our court to the Margrave, an officer waited on the D— of H—— and conducted us to the palace.

There

There were at dinner the reigning Prince and Princefs;—three of their fons, the eldeft of whom is married to a Princefs of Heffe Darmftadt.—She with one of her fifters was prefent, alfo the Princefs Dowager of Bareith, daughter to the Duke of Brunfwick; two general officers in the Imperial fervice, and other ladies and gentlemen, making in all a company of above thirty at table.

The entertainment was fplendid.—The Margrave behaved with the politeft attention to the D— of H——, and with affability to every body.

The Princefs of Bareith is of a gay, lively, agreeable character. After dinner the Duke took a view of the different apartments of the palace, and afterwards walked with the Margrave in the gardens till the evening.

The fame company were at fupper; a band of mufic played during the repaft, and the day went off in a more eafy, agreeable manner than I could have expected, confidering the number of Princes and Princeffes.

The Margrave of Baden Durlach is between forty and fifty years of age. He is a man of learning, good fenfe, and benevolent difpofitions. I had heard much, long before I faw him, of his humanity and attention to the well-being of his fubjects. This made me view him with a cordial regard, which his rank alone could not have commanded.

He fpeaks the Englifh language with confiderable facility, and is well acquainted with our beft authors. Solicitous that his fon fhould enjoy the fame advantages, he has engaged Mr. Cramer, a young gentleman from Scotland, of an excellent character, who

who has been for feveral years at this court
as tutor and companion to the young Prince.

The German Princes are minute obfervers
of form. The fame eftablifhment for their
houfehold, the fame officers in the palace,
are to be found here, as in the court of the
moft powerful monarch in Europe.—The
difference lies more in the falaries than in
the talents requifite for thefe places; one
Paymafter for the forces has greater emolu-
ments in England, than a Grand Marechal,
a Grand Chamberlain, two Secretaries of
State, and half a dozen more of the chief
officers of a German court, all taken together.

The Margrave of Baden has body guards
who do duty in the palace, foot guards who
parade before it; alfo horfe guards and huf-
fars, all of whom are perfectly well equipped
and exactly difciplined;—a piece of magnificence which feems to be adopted by
this

this prince, merely in conformity with the cuſtom long eſtabliſhed in his country.

He keeps on foot no other troops beſides the few which are neceſſary for this duty at the palace, though his revenue is more conſiderable, and his finances are in much better order than ſome Princes in Germany who have little ſtanding armies in conſtant pay. He has too juſt an underſtanding not to perceive that the greateſt army he could poſſibly maintain, could be no defence to his dominions, ſituated as they are between the powerful ſtates of France and Auſtria: And probably his principles and difpoſitions prevent him from thinking of filling his coffers by hiring his ſubjects to foreign powers.

If he were ſo inclined, there is no manner of doubt that he might ſell the perſons of his ſubjects as ſoldiers, or employ them in any other way he ſhould think proper; for he, as well as the other ſovereign Princes

ces in Germany, has an unlimited power over his people. If you ask the question, in direct terms, of a German, he will answer in the negative; and will talk of certain rights which the subjects enjoy, and that they can appeal to the great council or general diet of the empire for relief. But after all his ingenuity and distinctions, you find that the barriers which protect the peasant from the power of the prince, are so very weak, that they are hardly worth keeping up, and that the only security the peasant has for his person or property, must proceed from the moderation, good sense, and justice of his sovereign.

Happy would it be for mankind if this unlimited power were always placed in as equitable hands as those of the Margrave of Baden, who employs it entirely for the good of his subjects, by whom he is adored!

This

This Prince endeavours, by every means he can devise, to introduce industry and manufactures among his people.—There is a considerable number of English tradesmen here, who make Birmingham work, and instruct the inhabitants in that business. He has also engaged many watch-makers from Geneva to settle here, by granting them encouragements and privileges of every kind, and allows no opportunity to slip unimproved, by which he can promote the comfort and happiness of his people: A prince of such a character is certainly a public blessing, and the people are fortunate who are born under his government: But far more fortunate they who are born under a government which can protect them, independent of the virtues, and in spite of the vices, of their sovereign.

When we left Karlsruch, the Margrave gave orders that we might be allowed to pass by a road lately finished, through a noble

noble foreſt, ſeveral leagues in length. After having traverſed this, we fell in with the common poſting road, entered the biſhop of Spires's territories, paſſed by the town of that name, proceeded to the Electorate of Palatine, and arrived the ſame night at Manheim.

All the countries I have mentioned form one rich fertile plain; there are few or no gentlemen's houſes to vary the ſcene; nothing but the palace of the prince and the cottages of the peaſants, the gentry living in dependence at court, and the merchants and manufacturers in the towns.

LETTER XLII.

Manheim.

THIS is generally reckoned one of the moſt beautiful cities in Germany. The ſtreets are all as ſtraight as arrows, being what they call tirées au cordeau, and interſect each other at right angles. This never fails to pleaſe at firſt, but becomes ſooner tireſome than a town built with leſs regularity. When a man has walked through the town for half a forenoon, his eyes ſearch in vain for variety: the ſame objects ſeem to move along with him, as if he had been all the while a ſhip-board.

They calculate the number of inhabitants at 24,000, including the garriſon, which conſiſts of 5000 men. This town has three noble gates, adorned with baſſo relievos very beautifully

beautifully executed. The Duke and I walked round the ramparts with eafe in the fpace of an hour. The fortifications are well contrived and in good order, and the town acquires great additional ftrength from being almoft entirely furrounded by the Neckar and the Rhine, and fituated in a flat, not commanded by any rifing ground. Yet perhaps it would be better that this city were quite open, and without any fortification. An attempt to defend it might prove the deftruction of the citizen's houfes, and the electoral palace. A palace is injudicioufly fituated when built within a fortified town, becaufe a threat from the enemy to bombard it, might induce the garrifon to furrender.

The Electoral palace is a moft magnificent ftructure, fituated at the junction of the Rhine and the Neckar.—The cabinet of natural curiofities, and the collection of pictures, are much vaunted. To examine them was

was amufing enough:—To defcribe them would, I fear, be a little tedious.

The Elector himfelf is a man of tafte and magnificence, circumftances in his character, which probably afford more pleafure to himfelf, and the ftrangers who pafs this way, than to his own fubjects.

I accompanied the D— to one of the officers of the court, whofe bufinefs it is to prefent ftrangers. This gentleman is remarkable for his amazing knowledge in all the myfteries of etiquette. He entertained his Grace with much erudition on this fubject.—I never obferved the D— yawn fo very much.—When our vifit was over, he afferted that it had lafted two hours.—Upon examining his watch, he difcovered that he had made a miftake of one hour and forty minutes only.

We were presented the following day to the Elector and the Electress. He was dressed in the uniform of his guards, seems to be on the borders of fifty, and has a sensible manly countenance, which I am told is the true index of his character.

The Hereditary Prince is a young man of knowledge and good sense. He surprised me by talking of the party-disputes and adventures which have happened of late years in England, of which I found him minutely informed.— Many people in Germany have the English news-papers and political pamphlets regularly transmitted to them. The acrimony and freedom with which the highest characters are treated, astonish and amuse them, and from these they often form very false and extraordinary conclusions with regard to the state of the nation.

As the Elector intends soon to visit Italy, great numbers of officers have come hither to pay their duty to their sovereign before he depart for that country. He is much esteemed by his officers, with whom he lives in a very affable manner. There are generally thirty covers every day at his table for them, and the strangers who happen to be at the court of Manheim.

One day at dinner, a kind of buffoon came into the room. He walked round the table, and conversed in a familiar manner with every body present, the princes not excepted. His observations were followed by loud bursts of applause from all whom he addressed. As he spoke in German, I could not judge of his wit, but stared around with the anxiety of countenance natural to a man who sees a whole company ready to die with laughter at a jest which he cannot comprehend. An old officer, who sat near me, was touched with compassion for my situation, and explained into French some of the moſt brilliant repartees for my private uſe.

As this good-natured officer did not ſeem to have a great command of the French language, the whole ſpirit of the jeſt was allowed to evaporate during the tranſlation:— At leaſt I could not ſmell a particle when the procefs was over. However, as theſe tranſlations evidently coſt him a good deal of trouble, I thought myſelf obliged to ſeem delighted with his performance; ſo I joined in the mirth of the company, and endeavoured to laugh as much as any perſon at the table.

My interpreter afterwards informed me that this genius was from the Tyrol, that he ſpoke the German with ſo peculiar an accent, that whatever he ſaid never failed to ſet the whole table in a roar; c'eſt pourquoi, added he, il eſt en poſſeſſion d'entrer toujours avec le deſert.

This

This is the only example that I know remaining of a court fool or licenfed jefter; an office formerly univerfal in all the courts of Europe.

LETTER XLIII.

Manheim.

WE made a fhort jaunt to Heidelberg a few days fince. That town is about four leagues from Manheim.

Heidelberg is fituated in a hollow on the banks of the Neckar, and is furrounded by charming hills perfectly cultivated.

More cheerful fcenes of exuberant fertility are to be feen no where than along the fine chain of hills which begin near this town. The fummits of thefe hills are crowned with trees, and their fides and bottoms are clothed with vines.

The Elector's caftle is placed on an eminence, which commands the town, and a
view

view of the valley below; but the caſtle itſelf unfortunately is commanded by another eminence too near it, from which this noble building was cannonaded when the whole Palatinate was pillaged and burnt, in conſequence of that cruel order of Lewis XIV. too literally executed by Turenne.

The particulars of that diſmal ſcene have been tranſmitted from father to ſon, and are ſtill ſpoke of with horror by the peaſantry of this country, among whom the French nation is held in deteſtation to this day.

While we were in the caſtle we did not omit viſiting the renowned Heidelberg tun; but as it was perfectly empty, it made but a dull and unintereſting appearance.

The inhabitants of the Palatinate are partly Proteſtants, and partly Roman Catholics, who live here in harmony with each other. The great church at Heidelberg is
divided

divided into two apartments, in one of which the Proteſtants, and in the other, the Papiſts, perform public worſhip:—A ſingular proof of the moderation and coolneſs of people's minds with regard to a ſubject that inflamed them ſo violently in the days of their anceſtors.

We remained only one day at Heidelberg, and returned in the evening to this place. The lives and manners of the inhabitants of this city ſeem to be as uniform and formal as the ſtreets and buildings. No noiſe, mobs or buſtle; at mid-day every thing is as calm and quiet as the ſtreets of London at midnight. This gives one the notion that the citizens are under the ſame reſtraint and diſcipline with the troops.

I have ſeen theſe laſt perform their exerciſe every morning on the parade. I was a good deal ſurpriſed to obſerve, that not only the movements of the ſoldiers muſkets, and

and the attitudes of their bodies, but also their devotions, were under the direction of the major's cane. The following motions are performed as part of the military manœuvres every day before the troops are marched to their different guards.

The major flourishes his cane;—the drum gives a single tap, and every man under arms raises his hand to his hat;—at a second stroke on the drum, they take off their hats, and are suppofed to pray;—at a third, they finish their petitions, and put their hats on their heads.—If any man has the assurance to prolong his prayer a minute longer than the drum indicates, he is punished on the spot, and taught to be less devout for the future.

The ingenious inventor of drums certainly never dreamt of their becoming the regulators of people's piety.—But the modern improvements in the military art are truly wonderful!—

derful!—and we need not defpair, after this, of feeing a whole regiment, by the progrefs of difcipline, fo modelled as to eat, drink, and perform other animal functions, uniformly together, at the word of command, as they poife their firelocks.

LETTER XLIV.

Manheim.

HAVING left orders at Geneva to forward all our letters of a certain date to Manheim, and to direct thofe which fhould come afterwards, to Frankfort on the Maine, I had the good fortune to receive yours laft night.

I feel as much indignation as you poffibly can, againft thofe who endeavour to hurt the peace of families by malignant publications, and I enter fully into Lord ——'s on fo unmerited an attack. Yet I fhould be heartily forry to fee thefe evils remedied by any reftriction on the freedom of the prefs; becaufe I am every day more and more convinced that its unreftrained productions, the licentious news-papers themfelves not excepted,

cepted, have conveyed to every corner of Great Britain, along with much impertinence and fcurrility, fuch a regard for the conftitution, fuch a fenfe of the rights of the fubject, and fuch a degree of general knowledge, as never were fo univerfally diffufed over any other nation. Such a law as your friend propofes might, no doubt, protect individuals from unjuft attacks in print: but it would at the fame time remove one great means of clearing their innocence, and making known their wrongs, when injured in a more effential manner. It would limit the right which every Briton has of publicly addreffing his countrymen, when he finds himfelf injured or oppreffed by the perverfion of law, or the infolence of office.

Examples might be given of men of great integrity being attacked in the moft cruel and ungenerous manner by people high in office and guarded by power. Such men had no other means of redrefs than that of appealing to the candour and good sense of the public, which they used with success. Every man's observation may suggest to him many kinds of injustice and oppression which the rich, the insidious, or the powerful, can commit in spite of law, or perhaps by the aid of law, against the poor, the unsuspecting, and the friendless.—Many, who can silence conscience and evade law, tremble at the thoughts of their injustice being published; and nothing is, nothing can be, a greater check to the wantonness of power, than the privilege of unfolding private grievances at the bar of the public. For thus the cause of individuals is made a public concern, and the general indignation which their wrongs excite, forms at once one of the severest punishments which can be inflicted on the oppressor, and one of the strongest bulwarks that can be raised in defence of the unprotected.

By this means also the most speedy and effectual alarm is given all over the nation when any great public misconduct happens, or upon any appearance of a design against the constitution; and many evils are detected and prevented, which otherwise might have been unobserved, till they had become too strong for remedy. And though this liberty produces much silly advice, and malignant censors without number, it likewise opens the door to some of a different character, who give useful hints to ministers, which would have been lost without the freedom of anonymous publication.

The temporary and partial disorders, which are the consequences of public freedom, have been greatly exaggerated by some people, and represented as more than equivalent to all the advantages resulting from a free government. But if such persons had opportunities of observing the nature of those evils

evils which spring up in absolute governments, they would soon be convinced of their error.

The greatest evil that can arise from the licentiousness which accompanies civil liberty is, that people may rashly take a dislike to liberty herself, from the teasing impertinence and absurdity of some of her real or affected well-wishers; as a man might become less fond of the company of his best friend, if he found him always attended by a snappish cur, which without provocation was always growling and barking.

But to prove the weakness of such conduct, we have only to call to mind that the stream of licentiousness perhaps never rose higher than it did some years since in England.—And what were the mighty evils that followed?—Many respectable characters were grossly misrepresented in printed publications.—Certain daring scribblers evaded the punishment they deserved :—Many windows were broken, and the chariots of a few members of parliament were bespattered with dirt by the mob.——What are these frivolous disorders when compared to the gloomy regularity produced by despotism ? in which men are obliged to the most painful circumspection in all their actions; are afraid to speak their sentiments on the most common occurrences; suspicious of cherishing government spies in their household servants; distrustful of their own relations and most intimate companions, and at all times exposed to the oppression of men in power, and to the insolence of their favourites ?—No confusion, in my mind, can be more terrible than the stern disciplined regularity and vaunted police of arbitrary governments, where every heart is depressed by fear, where mankind dare not assume their natural characters, where the free spirit must crouch to the slave in office, where genius must repress her effusions, or

like

like the Egyptian worshippers, offer them in sacrifice to the calves of power; and where the human mind, always in shackles, shrinks from every generous effort.

LETTER XLV.

Mentz.

WE left Manheim five or six days ago.

It is very easy travelling through this part of Germany, the roads being perfectly good, and the country a continued plain. From Basil to within a few miles of Mentz, the posting road does not make even the most gentle ascent; a vast length of country to be all along a perfect level.

By the great numbers of Monks and Friars, of all colours and conditions, that are to be met near this city, we were apprised of our entrance into an ecclesiastical state, while the plump persons and rosy complexions of these Fathers sufficiently proved, that they did not live in the fertile land of Rhenish for nothing.

However

However good Chriftians they might be, many of them had much the appearance of paying occafional homage to the ancient heathen deity Bacchus, without being reftrained in their worfhip like the foldiers on the parade at Manheim.—One of them in particular appeared to have juft arifen from his devotion.—He moved along in the moft unconcerned manner imaginable, without obferving any direct courfe, or regarding whether he went to the right hand or to the left. He muttered to himfelf as he went.—Does he repeat his pater-nofter? faid I.—I rather imagine he prays from Horace, replied the D——

—— Quo me, Bacche, rapis tui
Plenum? Quæ nemora, aut quos agor in
  fpecus
Velox mente nova?——

On both fides of the Rhine the ground here begins to become hilly and irregular, forming

forming banks finely expofed to the fun. Here the beft Rhenifh wine is produced, and even a very fmall portion of thefe exuberant banks is of confiderable value. A chain of well-inhabited villages runs along from Mentz, by Bacharach, all the way to Coblentz, where the Rhine is joined by the Mofelle.

Bacharach is faid to derive its name from an altar of Bacchus (Bacchi Ara) fuppofed to have been erected by the Romans in gratitude for the quantity and quality of the wine produced in the neighbourhood. A little before we entered Mentz, we paffed by the Favorita, a beautiful palace belonging to the Elector, fituated where the Rhine is joined by the Maine.

Mentz is finely fituated, built in an irregular manner, and moft plentifully provided with churches. The cathedral is but a gloomy fabric. In this there is what they

they call a treasury, which contains a number of clumsy jewels, some relics, and a mighty rich wardrobe of priests vestments.

There are some troops in this capital, but I do not think the officers have that smart presumptuous air which generally accompanies men of their profession. They seem conscious that the clergy are their masters; and, I have a notion, are a little out of countenance on that account.

The streets swarm with ecclesiastics, some of them in fine coaches, and attended by a great number of servants. I remarked also many genteel airy abbes; who, one could easily see, were the most fashionable people, and give the ton at this place.

Though it is most evident that in this electorate the clergy have taken exceeding good care of themselves; yet, in justice to them,

them, it muſt be acknowledged, that the people alſo ſeem to be in an eaſy ſituation. The peaſantry appear to be in a ſtate of far greater abundance than thoſe of France, or even thoſe in the Elector of Manheim's dominions.

I have ſome deſire to ſee an eccleſiaſtical court, and would willingly viſit this of Mentz; but the D—— of H——, who ſeems to have no exceſſive fondneſs for any court, ſays, a court of clergymen muſt be more diſmal and tedious than any other, and I fear will not be prevailed on to appear at this; in which caſe we will leave this place to-morrow morning early, without further ceremony.

LETTTER XLVI.

Frankfort on the Maine.

WE have been here two weeks.—To form a proper judgment of the genius and manners of any nation, it is neceſſary to live familiarly with the inhabitants for a conſiderable time; but a ſmaller degree of obſervation will ſuffice to give a pretty juſt idea of the nature of its government. The chilling effects of deſpotic oppreſſion, or the benign influence of freedom and commerce, ſtrike the eye of the moſt careleſs traveller.

The ſtreets of Frankfort are ſpacious and well-paved; the houſes ſtately, clean, and convenient, the ſhops well furniſhed; the dreſs, the numbers, the air, and general manners

manners of the inhabitants, sufficiently show, without other information, that there is no little despot within their walls, to impoverish them in support of his grandeur, and to put every action of their lives, every movement of their bodies, under restraint by his caprice.

The houses are of brick, but have a better appearance than brick houses in general, owing chiefly to their being covered with a kind of reddish stucco, which is come into use here of late, and, it is believed, will render the buildings more durable. The fronts of many of the finest are also adorned with bas reliefs, of white stucco, in imitation of marble. These white ornaments, on the red ground, form too strong a contrast, and do not please an eye fond of simplicity. But the Germans, in general, have a taste for showy ornament, in their dress, furniture, and houses. Frankfort is a free imperial city, having a
small

small territory belonging to it, and is governed by its own magiſtracy.

All religions are tolerated here, under certain reſtrictions; but Lutheraniſm is the eſtabliſhed faith, as the magiſtrates are of that communion.

The principal church is in the poſſeſſion of the Roman Catholics, but no public proceſſiom of the hoſt is permitted through the ſtreets. All the ceremonies of their religion are confined to the houſes of individuals, or performed within the walls of this church. In it there is a chapel, to which the Emperor is conducted immediately after his election, in order to be crowned by the Elector of Mentz.

The Jews have a ſynagogue in this city, where they perform their religious rites; but the Calviniſts have never been allowed any public houſe of worſhip within the territory

ritory of Frankfort. They attend divine service at a place called Bockenheim in the county of Hanau, where they have built a church.

This is but unkind treatment; and it seems, at first sight, a little extraordinary, that Martin Luther should show more indulgence to his old enemy Lord Peter, and even to Judas Iscariot himself, than to his fellow reformer John Calvin.

Though Frankfort is thought a fine town, and the effect produced by the whole is magnificent, yet there are no buildings in particular worthy of attention. It is expected, however, that all strangers should visit the town-house, and see the chamber where the Emperor is elected. And it would be reckoned a great want of curiosity, not to see the famous golden bull which is kept there with the utmost care. A sight of this costs a golden ducat; a sufficient

ficient price for a glance of an old manuscript, which not one perfon in a hundred can read, and ftill fewer can underftand.

A countryman of ours, who expected more amufement for his money, complained loudly of this as an impofition, and on hearing a German talk of the high price which every thing bore in England, he retorted on him in thefe words:—Il n'y a rien en Amgleterre fi cher que votre *taureau* d'or a Framkfort.

There is a cuftom obferved here, which I fhall mention on account of its fingularity, though I enquired in vain for its origin. Two women appear every day at noon on the battlements of the principal fteeple, and play fome very folemn airs with trumpets. This mufic is accompanied by vocal pfalmody, performed by four or five men, who always attend the female trumpeters for that purpofe.

The

The people here have a violent taste for psalm-singing. There are a considerable number of men and boys, who have this for their only profession. They are engaged by some families to officiate two or three times a week in the morning, before the master and mistress of the family get out of bed.

When any person in tolerable circumstances dies, a band of these sweet singers assemble in the streets before the house, and chant an hour every day to the corpse, till it is interred. The same band accompanies the funeral, singing hymns all the way.

Funerals are conducted with an uncommon degree of solemnity in this town:— A man clothed in a black cloak, and carrying a crucifix, at the end of a long pole, leads the procession:—A great number of hired mourners in the same dress, and each

with

with a lemon in his hand, march after him:—Then come the fingers, followed by the corpſe in a hearſe; and laſtly, the relations in mourning coaches.

The crucifix is carried in this manner at all funerals, whether the deceaſed has died a Roman Catholic, a Lutheran, or a Calviniſt. That this cuſtom ſhould be followed by the two latter, ſurpriſed me a good deal. I ſhould have imagined that the Calviniſts in particular, whatever they did with the lemons, would never have been able to digeſt the crucifix.

There is a very conſiderable number of Calviniſts in this place; it is generally thought they are the moſt induſtrious. They unqueſtionably are the richeſt part of the inhabitants. This may be partly owing to a circumſtance that ſome of them conſider as a hardſhip——their being excluded from any ſhare in the government of the city.—Many of the Calvinist families are descendents of French Protestants, who left their country at the revocation of the edict of Nantz.

There are some villages near Frankfort consisting entirely of French refugees; who, deserting their country at the same time, have settled here in a cluster. Their descendents speak French in their common conversation, and retain many of their original customs to this hour.

Two or three families now living at Frankfort are of English origin. Their predecessors fled first to Holland, during the persecutions in the reign of Mary, and being afterwards driven out of that country by the cruelty of the Duke of Alva, they at length found an asylum for themselves, and their posterity, in this free imperial city.

The

The number of Jews in Frankfort is prodigious, confidering one difmal inconvenience they are fubjected to, being obliged to live all together in a fingle ftreet built up at one end :—There is a large gate at the other, which is regularly fhut at a certain hour of the night, after which no Jews dare appear in the ftreets; but the whole herd muft remain cooped and crowded together, like fo many black cattle, till morning. As this ftreet is narrow, the room allotted for each family fmall, and as the children of Ifrael were never remarkable for their cleanlinefs, and always noted for breeding, the Jews quarter, you will believe, is not the fweeteft part of the town. I fcarce think they could have been worfe lodged in the land of Egypt.

They have feveral times made offer of confiderable fums to the magiftrates of Frankfort for liberty to build or purchafe another street for their accommodation; but all such proposals have hitherto been rejected.

The Jews in Frankfort are obliged to fetch water when a fire happens in any part of the city, and the magistrates in return permit them to choose judges out of their own body for deciding disputes among themselves; but if either party refuses to submit to this, an appeal is open to the magistrates.

They must unquestionably enjoy some great advantages by the trade they carry on, to compensate for such inconveniencies. During the day-time they are allowed the liberty of walking all over the town; a privilege which they improve with equal assiduity and address. They attack you in the street, ply at the gate of your lodgings, and even glide into your apartments, offering to supply you with every commodity you

you can have occasion for: And if you happen to pass by the entrance of their street, they intreat your custom with the violence and vociferation of so many Thames watermen.

I was twice at their synagogue. There is nothing magnificent in their worship; but much apparent zeal and fervour. I saw one of their most important rites performed on two children. It was impossible not to feel compassion for the poor infants, thus cruelly initiated into a community, who had formerly the misfortune of being despised by the Heathens, and now are execrated by all pious Christians.

LETTER XLVII.

Frankfort on the Maine.

YOU will be furprifed at our remaining fo long at a place where there is no court, and few of thofe entertainments which allure and retain travellers. The truth is, the D— of H—— feems fond of this place; and as for my own part, I have formed an acquaintance with fome very worthy people here, whofe friendfhip I fhall take every occafion to cultivate.

Society here is divided into Nobleffe and the Bourgeois. The firft confifts of fome noble families from various parts of Germany, who have chofen Frankfort for their refidence, and a few original citizens of Frankfort, but who have now obtained the rank of nobility. The citizens who connect

nect themſelves with ſtrangers, have made their fortunes by commerce, which ſome of them ſtill follow.

There is a public aſſembly for the nobility once a week, at which they drink tea, converſe, or play at cards from ſix to ten. On the other nights, the ſame company meet alternately at each other's houſes, and paſs the evening in the ſame manner. None of the Bourgeois families are invited to theſe parties, but they have aſſemblies of the ſame kind among themſelves, and often entertain their friends and the ſtrangers with whom they are acquainted, in a very hoſpitable manner at their tables. The noblemen who reſide in Frankfort, and the nobility of all degrees, and of every nation, who accidentally paſs through it, cheerfully accept of theſe invitations to dine with the citizens, but none of the German ladies of quality condeſcend ſo far. While their fathers, huſbands, and brothers, are entertained at a Bourgeois table,

table, they chufe rather to dine at home by themfelves; and they certainly judge wifely, if they prefer a fpare diet to good cheer.

The diftinction of ranks is obferved in Germany, with all the fcrupulous precifion that a matter of that importance deferves. There is a public concert in this place fupported by fubfcription. One would imagine that the fubfcribers would take their feats as they entered the room, that thofe who came earlieft would have their choice.—No fuch matter.—The two firft rows are kept for the ladies of quality, and the wives and daughters of the citizens muft be contented to fit behind, let them come at what hour, and pay what money they pleafe.—After all, this is not fo bad as in an affembly of nobility, where commons are not permitted to fit, even in the lobby, whatever price they may have paid for their feat in parliament.

Since

Since we arrived, the theatre has been opened for the winter, by a troop of German comedians. I was there the firſt night; previous to the play, there was a kind of allegorical prologue, intended as a compliment to the magiſtrates of Frankfort. This was performed by Juſtice, Wiſdom, and Plenty, each of whom appeared in perſon, with the uſual attributes. The laſt was very properly perſonated by a large fat woman, big with child. As to the two former, I hope, for the ſake of the good people of Frankfort, that they are better repreſented in the town-council, than they were on the ſtage. This prologue was concluded by a long harangue pronounced by the plumpeſt Apollo, I dare venture to ſay, that ever appeared in the heavens above, or on the earth beneath.

After this the play began, which was a German tranſlation of the Engliſh play of George Barnwell, with conſiderable alterations.

tions. Barnwell is reprefented as an imprudent young man; but he does not murder his uncle, as in the Englifh play, or commit any grofs crime; the German tranflator therefore, inftead of hanging, only marries him at the end of the piece.

Moft of the plays reprefented on the German ftage, are tranflations from the Englifh or French; for Germany, fo fertile in writers in divinity, jurifprudence, medicine, chymiftry, and other parts of natural philofophy, has produced few poets till of late,

Jam nova progenies cœlo demittitur alto,

and the German mufe is now admired all over Europe. Her beauties are felt and applauded by men of genius, even through the medium of a tranflation, which is a ftrong proof of her original energy. It muft, however, be a great difcouragement to German poetry in general, and to the dramatic in particular, that the French language prevails in all the courts, and that French plays are reprefented there in preference to German.

The native language of the country is treated like a vulgar and provincial dialect, while the French is cultivated as the only proper language for people of fafhion.—Children of the firft families are inftructed in French, before they acquire their mother-tongue, and pains are taken to keep them ignorant of this, that it may not hurt their pronunciation of the other. I have met with people who confidered it as an accomplifh-ment to be unable to exprefs themfelves in the language of their country, and who have pretended to be more ignorant, in this particular, than they were in reality.

I have been affured by many, who underftand the German language well, that it is nervous, copious, moft expreffive, and capable of all the graces of poetry. The truth of this appears by the works of feveral late writers,

writers, who have endeavoured to check this unnatural prejudice in their countrymen, and to restore the language of their ancestors to its native honours.—But what are the efforts of good sense, taste, and genius, in opposition to fashion, and the influence of courts?

Among the winter amusements of this place, traineau parties may be reckoned. These can take place in the time of frost only, and when there is a considerable quantity of snow upon the ground. I had an opportunity of seeing a very splendid entertainment of this kind lately, which was given by some young gentlemen to an equal number of ladies.

A traineau is a machine in the shape of a horse, lion, swan; or in that of a griffin, unicorn, or some other fanciful form, without wheels; but made below like a sledge, for the conveniency of sliding over the snow.
Some

Some are gilded, and otherwife ornamented, according to the whim of the proprietor.—A pole ftands up from one fide, to which an enfign or flag is faftened, which waves over the heads of thofe placed on the machine. The lady, wrapped in fur, fits before, and the gentleman ftands behind on a board made for that purpofe.

The whole is drawn by two horfes, which are either conducted by a poftillion, or driven by the gentleman.—The horfes are gaudily ornamented, and have bells hanging from the trappings which cover them.

This party confifted of about thirty traineaus, each attended by two or three fervants on horfeback with flambeaux; for this amufement was taken when it began to grow dark.—One traineau took the lead;— the reft followed at a convenient diftance in a line, and drove for two or three hours through the principal ftreets and fquares of Frankfort.

Frankfort.—The horses go at a brisk trot or canter; the motion of the traineau is easy and agreeable; the bells, ensigns, and torches, make a very gay and showy appearance, which seemed to be much relished by the parties immediately concerned, and admired by the spectators.

A few days after this exhibition, as we were preparing to set out for Hanau in a traineau, Mr. S——, brother to Lord S——, arrived at the inn. Though he had travelled for two days and nights, without having been in bed, he was so little fatigued, that he went along with us. Hanau is some leagues distant from Frankfort. We had a full proof of the fine easy motion of the traineau, which, in the time of frost, and when there is a proper quantity of snow on the ground, is certainly the most delightful way of travelling that can possibly be imagined.

Hanau

Hanau is the residence of the Hereditary Prince of Hesse Cassel. As we entered the town we met the Princess, who is sister-in-law to the King of Denmark. She, with some of the ladies of the court, was taking the air also in a traineau.

Besides the troops of Hanau, two regiments of Hanoverians are there at present. The Hereditary Prince is not on the best terms with his father. He lives here, however, in a state of independency, possessed of the revenues of this county, which is guaranteed to him by the Kings of Britain, Denmark, and Prussia: but there is no intercourse between this little court and that of Hesse Cassel.

After dinner we returned to Frankfort. The D— prevailed with Mr. S— to remain a longer time at Frankfort than he had intended. He is a sensible young man of spirit and ambition. His grandfather, the old Earl

Earl of D——, endeavours to seduce him into holy orders, promising him a living of 2000l. a year, which is in the gift of the family. This you will acknowledge to be a temptation which few younger brothers could withstand. Nature, however, seems to have destined this young gentleman for another line in life. My own opinion is, he would rather have the command of a troop of dragoons, than be promoted to the See of Canterbury.

LETTER XLVIII.

Frankfort.

SOME of the nobility who reside in this city, take every opportunity of pointing out the essential difference that there is, and the distinctions that ought to be made, between their families and those of the Bourgeois, who, though they have, by commerce or some profession equally ignoble, attained great wealth, which enables them to live in a stile of magnificence unbecoming their rank; yet their noble neighbours insinuate, that they always retain a vulgarity of sentiment and manners, unknown to those whose blood has flowed pure through several generations, unmixed with that puddle which stagnates in the veins of plebeians.

The D— of H— does not seem to have studied natural philosophy with accuracy sufficient to enable him to observe this distinction. He mingles in the societies of the citizens, with as much ease and alacrity, as in those of the nobility, dining with the one, and drinking coffee with the other, in the most impartial manner, and between the two he contrives to amuse himself tolerably well.

The two families with which we are in the greatest degree of intimacy, are those of Monf. de Barkhaufe, and Monf. P. Gogle. The former is a principal person in the magistracy, a man of learning and worth. His lady is of a noble family in the dukedom of Brunswic, a woman of admirable good sense and many accomplishments. She is well acquainted with English and French literature. The French language she speaks like a native, and though she cannot converse in Englifh without difficulty, fhe underftands and relifhes the works of fome of our beft authors.

Mr. Gogle has travelled over the greateft part of Europe, and is equally acquainted with men and books. He has made a plentiful fortune by commerce, and lives in a very agreeable and hofpitable manner.

In thefe two houfes we occafionally meet with the beft company of both the claffes of fociety in this place, and in one or other when there is no public affembly we generally pafs the afternoon.—The former part of the day (a thaw having lately diffolved the fnow) we often pafs in jaunts to the environs of this place, which are very beautiful.

As the D— of H—— and I were riding one day along the banks of the Maine, near the village of Heix, which is in the territories of the Elector of Mentz, we obferved a

building

building which seemed to be the residence of some prince, or bishop at least. We were surprised we never had heard it spoken of, as it had a more magnificent appearance than any modern building we had seen since our arrival in Germany. We rode up, and upon entering it, found that the apartments within, though not laid out in the best taste, seemed to correspond, in point of expence, with the external appearance.

We were informed by the workmen, who were employed in finishing these apartments, that this palace belonged to a tobacconist in Frankfort, where he still kept shop, and had accumulated a prodigious fortune by making and selling snuff.

Near to the principal house, there is another great building intended for a workhouse, in which tobacco is to be manufactured, with many apartments for the workmen, and vaulted cellars in which the various

various kinds of snuff are to be kept moist, till sent for inland sale to Frankfort, or shipped on the Maine for foreign markets.

The owner informed us, there were exactly three hundred rooms in both buildings, and the greater number of these belonged to the dwelling-house. We did not chuse to puzzle the man by difficult questions, and therefore refrained from enquiring, what use he intended to make of such an amazing number of rooms, which seemed rather contrived as barracks for two or three thousand soldiers, than any other purpose.

On our return to town, we were informed that this person, who is not a native of Frankfort, though he has been many years established there, had applied to the magistrates for liberty to purchase a certain spot of ground, on which he proposed to build a dwelling-house, &c. which cannot be done by any but citizens, without the consent of the council. This being refufed, he bought a little piece of land in the territory of Mentz, immediately beyond that of Frankfort, and on the banks of the Maine; and being highly piqued by the refufal he had met with from the magiftrates, he had reared a building greatly larger and more extenfive than was neceffary, or than he at firft had intended, in the full perfuafion that the remorfe of the magiftrates would be in proportion to the fize of this fabric.

The tobacconift has already expended fifty thoufand pounds on this temple of vengeance, and his wrath againft the magiftrates feems to be yet unappeafed—for he ftill lavifhes his money with a rancour againft thefe unfortunate men, that is very unbecoming a Chriftian. The inhabitants of Frankfort, while they acknowledge the imprudence of the magiftrates, do not applaud the wifdom of their antagonift, in whofe brain they affert there muft be fome

apartments

apartments as empty as any in the vaft ftructure he is building.

Another day his Grace and I rode to Bergen, a fmall village which has been rendered eminent by the attempt made there by Prince Ferdinand on the French army in the year 1759.

We were accompanied by the Meffrs. de Leffener, two gentlemen, now retired from the fervice, and living at Frankfort, who had been in the action, one a Captain in the Hanoverian army, the other of the fame rank in the French.

During the winter of that memorable year, you may remember that the French, with more policy than juftice, had feized upon this neutral city, and eftablifhed their head-quarters here. This was attended by great advantages, fecuring to them the courfe of the Maine and Upper Rhine, by which they

they received supplies from Strasburg, and all the intermediate cities.

Prince Ferdinand having formed the design of driving them from this advantageous situation, before they could be reinforced, suddenly assembled his army, which was cantoned about Munster, and after three days of forced marches, came in sight of the French army, at that time commanded by the Duke de Broglio, who, having received intelligence of the Prince's scheme, had made a very judicious disposition.

On the forenoon of the 13th of April, the Prince began his attack on the right wing of the French army, which occupied the village of Bergen.—This was renewed with great vivacity three several times. The Prince of Isembourg, and about 1500 of the Allies, fell in the action, which was prolonged till the evening; Prince Ferdinand then determining to draw off his troops,

troops, made such a disposition as convinced the enemy he intended a general attack next morning—and by this means he accomplished his retreat in the night, without being harassed by the French.

I have heard officers of great merit assert, that nothing could be more judiciously planned and executed, than this enterprise; the only one of importance, however, in which that great General failed during the whole war.

By this misfortune the allied army were reduced to great difficulties, and the progress of the French, with the continued retreat of the Allies, spread such an alarm over the Electorate of Hanover, that many individuals sent their most valuable effects to Stade, from whence they might be conveyed to England. — The affairs of the Allies were soon after re-established by the decisive victory of Minden, which raised the military character
of

of Prince Ferdinand higher than ever; though officers of penetration, who were at both actions, are still of opinion, that his talents were to the full as conspicuous at Bergen, where he was repulsed, as at the glorious field of Minden, by which Hanover and Brunswick were preserved, and the French obliged to abandon almost all Westphalia.

LETTER XLIX.

Frankfort.

I Returned a few days since from Darmstadt, having accompanied the D— of H—— on a visit which he made to that court.

The reigning Prince of Hesse Darmstadt not being there, we were directed to pay our first visit to the Princess Maximilian, his aunt.—She invited us the same evening to play at cards and sup with her.—There were about ten people at table.—The Princess was gay, affable, and talkative.—The D— confessed he never had passed an evening so agreeably with an old woman in his life.

Next morning we went to the parade, which is an object of great attention at this place. The Prince has a moſt enthuſiaſtic paſſion for military manœuvres and evolutions.—Drilling and exerciſing his ſoldiers are his chief amuſements, and almoſt his ſole employment. That he may enjoy this in all kinds of weather, and at every ſeaſon of the year, he has built a room ſufficiently capacious to admit 1500 men, to perform their exerciſe in it all together.

This room is accommodated with ſixteen ſtoves, by which it may be kept at the exact degrees of temperature which ſuits his Highneſs's conſtitution.—On the morning that we were preſent, there was only the ordinary guard, conſiſting of three hundred men, who having performed their exerciſes, and marched for an hour up and down this ſpacious Gymnaſium, were divided into parties and detached to their reſpective poſts.

The

The Darmſtadt ſoldiers are tall, tolerably clothed, and above all things remarkably well powdered. They go through their manœuvres with that dexterity which may be expected of men who are continually employed in the ſame action, under the eye of their prince, who is an admirable judge, and ſevere critic in this part of the military art.

There is no regular fortification round this town; but a very high ſtone-wall, which is not intended to prevent an enemy from entering, being by no means adequate to ſuch a purpoſe; but merely deſigned to hinder the garriſon from deſerting, to which they are exceedingly inclined; theſe poor men taking no delight in the warlike amuſements which conſtitute the ſupreme joy of their ſovereign.

Centinels are placed at ſmall diſtances all round the wall, who are obliged to be exceedingly

ceedingly alert. One foldier gives the words *all is well* in German, to his neighbour on the right, who immediately calls the fame to the centinel beyond him, and fo it goes round till the firft foldier receives the words from the left, which he tranfmits to the right as formerly, and fo the call circulates without any intermiffion through the whole night.

Every other part of garrifon duty is performed with equal exactnefs, and all neglects as feverely punifhed as if an enemy were at the gates.

The men are feldom more than two nights out of three in bed. This, with the attention requifite to keep their clothes and accoutrements clean, is very hard duty, efpecially at prefent, when the froft is uncommonly keen, and the ground covered with fnow.

There

There is a small body of cavalry at Darmstadt just now. They are dressed in buff coats, and magnificently accoutred.—These are the horse-guards of the prince.—Few as they are, I never saw so many men together of such a height, in my life, none of them being under six English feet three inches high, and several of them considerably above that enormous stature.

The Prince of Hesse Darmstadt formerly kept a greater number of troops: At present his whole army does not exceed five thousand men. But as the conduct of princes, however judicious it may be, seldom passes uncensured, there are people who blame him for entertaining even this number. They declare, that this prince's finances, being in very great disorder, cannot support this establishment; which, though small, may be counted high, considering the extent of his dominions. They insist also upon the loss,

loſs, which agriculture and manufactures muſt ſuſtain, by having the ſtouteſt men taken away from theſe neceſſary employments, and their ſtrength exhauſted in uſeleſs parade. For theſe rigid cenſors have the aſſurance to aſſert, that an army of five thouſand men, though burdenſome to the country, is not ſufficient to defend it; that the number is by far too great for amuſement, and infinitely too ſmall for any manner of uſe.

The ſame day, we dined with the Princeſs Maximilian, and in the afternoon were preſented to Prince George's family. He is brother to the reigning Prince. He happened to be indiſpoſed; but his princeſs received the D— with the utmoſt politeneſs.

Their two youngeſt ſons and three daughters were at ſupper. The former are ſtill very young; the latter are well-looking,

looking, remarkably accomplifhed, and do much credit to the great pains their mother has beftowed on their education.

Next morning we were invited to breakfaft, by the Baron Riedefal, at a pleafant country-houfe he has near Darmftadt.— His G— went with him, in a carriage of a very particular conftruction. The Baron fat on a low feat next the horfes, and drove; the D—— in a higher place behind him. Each of thefe is made for one perfon only; but behind all, there was a wooden feat, in the fhape of a little horfe, on which two fervants were mounted. The ufual pofting-chaifes in this country hold fix perfons with eafe; and people even of the firft rank generally have two or three fervants in the chaife with them. In point of œconomy, thefe carriages are well imagined; and, in the time of froft, not inconvenient; for here travellers take fpecial care to fortify themfelves againft cold by cloaks lined with fur. But when it rains hard, two of the company at leaſt muſt be drenched; for the German chaiſes are never intirely covered above.

I went with Count Cullemberg in his coach. We paſſed the forenoon very agreeably at this houſe, which ſeems to be advantageouſly ſituated; but in its preſent ſnowy dreſs, one can no more judge of the natural complexion of the country, than of that of an actreſs new-painted for the ſtage.

We dined with Prince George, who was ſufficiently recovered to be at table. He is a handſome man, of a ſoldier-like appearance, and has all the eaſe and openneſs of the military character.

His ſecond ſon, who had been abſent for ſome weeks, arrived while we were at table. He is a fine young man, about eighteen years of age. It was pleaſing to obſerve the satisfaction which this small incident diffused over the faces of father, mother, and the whole family, which formed a groupe worthy the pencil of Greuse.

Do not suspect that I am prejudiced in favour of this family, merely because they belong to a prince.——An appearance of domestic happiness is always agreeable, whether we find them in a palace or a cottage; and the same symptoms of good humour, though they would not have surprized me so much, would have delighted me equally in the family of a peasant.

END OF THE FIRST VOLUME.

www.ingramcontent.com/pod-product-compliance
Lightning Source LLC
Chambersburg PA
CBHW022101300426
44117CB00007B/548